John Sharry
Brendan Madden
Melissa Darmody

Becoming a Solution Detective
Identifying Your Clients' Strengths
in Practical Brief Therapy

Pre-publication
REVIEWS,
COMMENTARIES,
EVALUATIONS . . .

"**I**t is not easy to write a good hands-on book about solution-focused therapy, which is precisely what the authors have managed to do. You will enjoy reading this book very much. It gives you enough ideas about the approach that you can actually start testing them in your work with clients right away."

Ben Furman
Author, *Solution Talk: It's Never Too Late to Have a Happy Childhood, Pickpockets on a Nudist Camp— The Systemic Revolution in Psychotherapy,* and *Solutions Stories*

───────────

"**B**ecoming a Solution Detective is a brilliant book. First of all, it is well written and so affords the pleasure any well-written book gives an interested reader. Second, it is tightly written, crisp, and to the point. Third, it addresses the serious subject of therapy with a humor and lightness that exactly reflects its regard for the immense strength and resilience that we human beings can call upon in times of distress and adversity.

Anyone can pick up this book and find out what solution-focused brief therapy is all about—and enjoy themselves in the process. 'Solution detectives' who pick up this book will also find a generosity of spirit, for within the book are all the materials needed to teach solution-focused brief therapy. I cannot think of a better place to start out from if you want to become a solution-focused brief therapist, or to visit if you have already made the journey."

Chris Iveson
Co-Founder, Brief Therapy Practice, London, United Kingdom

More pre-publication
REVIEWS, COMMENTARIES, EVALUATIONS . . .

"**I**magine you and your clients as Sherlock Holmes and Dr. Watson carefully, thoughtfully, and creatively sleuthing together toward strengths and client solutions. This is what these authors delightfully dramatize as a metaphor of solution-focused work. In six simple chapters, Sharry, Madden, and Darmody capture and present the heart of the approach, and through suggested exercises provide opportunities to experience this approach firsthand. Novices will love this book for its simplicity and straightforwardness. Experienced people will relish the humor and the helpful teaching guides."

John Walter, MSW
Co-Author, *Recreating Brief Therapy: Preferences and Possibilities*

"**B**ecoming a Solution Detective* is an excellent introduction to solution-focused therapy, and much more. It takes readers, step by step, through the very processes a strengths-based therapist might offer a client. Using exercises and brief case studies as well as a bit of theory and some clever cartoons, readers get the invaluable learning experience of looking at themselves through 'solution lenses.' Very well done!"

Michael F. Hoyt, PhD
Author, *Some Stories Are Better Than Others, Brief Therapy and Managed Care, Interviews with Brief Therapy Experts,* and *The Present Is a Gift*

"**I**t's a miracle! An upbeat, practice-oriented book on solution-focused brief therapy that will be useful to newcomers to the model as well as to seasoned solution-focused practitioners and trainers. Sharry, Madden, and Darmody, with the help of Sherlock Holmes, clearly and systematically show therapists the practical how-to's for tackling a wide range of clients presenting difficulties using their expanded and flexible solution-focused therapy approach. The authors' compassion and respect for their clients' expertise and resourcefulness shines through on every page.

An added bonus feature of this well-written book is the numerous skill-building exercises the authors provide to help readers more quickly master the major therapeutic strategies and techniques of the approach. Supervisors and trainers will find these exercises quite useful in supervision meetings and workshop settings. *Becoming a Solution Detective* gets my vote as being one of the best solution-focused practice-oriented books on the market."

Matthew D. Selekman, MSW
Partners for Collaborative Solutions, Evanston, IL; Author,
Living on the Razor's Edge: Solution-Oriented Brief Therapy with Self-Harming Adolescents, and *Solution-Focused Therapy with Children: Harnessing Family Strengths for Systemic Change*

"**I**llustrated with interesting case examples, witty cartoons, and delightful literary quotes, this imaginative view of solution-focused brief therapy will appeal to beginners as well as experienced clinicians. Read and enjoy!"

Yvonne Dolan, MA
Psychotherapist;
Author; Trainer,
Solution-Focused Brief Therapy

The Haworth Clinical Practice Press
An Imprint of The Haworth Press, Inc.
New York • London • Oxford

Becoming a Solution Detective
Identifying Your Clients' Strengths in Practical Brief Therapy

HAWORTH Marriage and the Family
Terry S. Trepper, PhD
Executive Editor

Becoming a Solution Detective
Identifying Your Clients' Strengths in Practical Brief Therapy

John Sharry
Brendan Madden
Melissa Darmody

The Haworth Clinical Practice Press
An Imprint of The Haworth Press, Inc.
New York • London • Oxford

Published by

The Haworth Clinical Practice Press, an imprint of The Haworth Press, Inc., 10 Alice Street, Binghamton, NY 13904-1580.

First published as *Becoming a Solution-Focused Detective: A Strengths-Based Guide to Brief Therapy.* © 2001 by Brief Therapy Press, London.

Client identities and circumstances have been changed to protect confidentiality.

Cover design by Marylouise E. Doyle.

Cartoons by John Byrne.

Library of Congress Cataloging-in-Publication Data

Sharry, John.
    Becoming a solution detective : identifying your clients' strengths in practical brief therapy / John Sharry, Brendan Madden, Melissa Darmody.
        p. ; cm.
    Includes bibliographical references and index.
    ISBN 0-7890-1833-0 (hard cover : alk. paper) — ISBN 0-7890-1834-9 (soft cover : alk. paper)
    1. Solution-focused brief therapy.
        [DNLM: 1. Psychotherapy, Brief—methods. 2. Problem Solving. WM 420.5.P5 S532b 2003] I. Madden, Brendan. II. Darmody, Melissa. III. Title.
RC489.S65 S528 2003
616.89'14—dc21

                                                                        2002153151

To our parents,
for making us aware of the possibilities

ABOUT THE AUTHORS

John Sharry, DPsych, is Principal Social Worker at the Department of Child and Family Psychiatry in the Mater Hospital and a Director of the Brief Therapy Group in Dublin. He is co-author and producer of *Parents Plus Programmes,* a book and video-based series that uniquely combines the traditional social learning ideas around behavior management with a solution-focused framework. Dr. Sharry is the author of two previous psychotherapy books, including *Solution-Focused Groupwork,* as well as a number of self-help books for parents and families, including *Parent Power: Bringing Up Responsible Children and Teenagers.*

Brendan Madden, MA, is a psychologist and therapist with extensive experience in the field of brief therapy and EAP counseling services. He is a Founding Director and Senior Trainer with the Brief Therapy Group training partnership, a leading provider of solution-focused brief therapy (SFBT) training. For the past six years he has developed and delivered SFBT training programs to mental health and social work teams in all the major health care and social services organizations in Ireland. Together with his colleagues he has published in national and international journals in the field of counseling and therapy.

Melissa Darmody, DPsych, is a counseling psychologist with ten years of experience in the development and delivery of EAP services in Ireland and abroad and is Clinical Director of EAP Solutions. She has an extensive background in working with abuse and trauma victims and has written several articles that incorporate solution-focused brief therapy into work with adult survivors of abuse and trauma.

CONTENTS

Foreword

When I started teaching solution-focused brief therapy in Finland with my colleague Tapani Ahola in the mid-1980s there simply were no textbooks or manuals that would describe, in jargon-free language and with engaging case vignettes, the basic principles of solution-focused therapy. Times have changed now. Currently, quite a few hands-on books discuss how to help clients find solutions to their problems in a solution-focused manner, some better than others. The book that you are now holding in your hands is better than others.

Presenting radical ideas needs to be done in a sympathetic fashion and this is precisely what the authors of this book have accomplished. They have found a way to avoid disturbing the reader with the feeling that the model being presented is a quick fix that anybody can learn by just attending one workshop or reading a fashionable book about the subject. No one would believe such nonsense. It is true that it is easy to learn the principles of solution-focused therapy but we all know that it takes years of practice to become proficient in utilizing those principles effectively in the face of the varied situations that we clinicians deal with in our daily work with clients.

If you are a student of psychotherapy, you will enjoy this book very much. It is just the right size and it gives you enough ideas about this approach to therapy that you can actually start testing them in your work with clients the next day.

If you are a professional psychotherapist reading this book you will be pleased to discover that this book is able to explain complicated psychological concepts with the kind of clarity that many such books don't possess.

If you are a person contemplating seeking therapy for a problem, please take my advice and don't read this book. With all the illustrative case examples and useful exercises provided in the text, you might be able to overcome your problem all on your own, and that would not be good for the business of psychotherapy.

Ben Furman, Psychiatrist
Helsinki, Finland

Preface

One of the great strengths of solution-focused therapy is its simplicity. de Shazer and the other originators of the model shared a concern to make the approach clear and concise and not overly cluttered with theory or intellectualization. The aim was to make psychotherapy brief and efficient both in theory and practice.

In our work in the Brief Therapy Group in Dublin, Ireland, we attempt to emulate these principles of simplicity and conciseness, both in our approach to therapeutic work and in how we teach the approach to others. In teaching, our aim is not to overly complicate the essence of psychotherapy with extra theory or over abstract ideas, but rather to demystify this process, making the ideas accessible and relevant to all. Indeed, we believe the benefits of a solution-focused approach to problem solving extend far beyond the limits of psychotherapy and counseling and have much to contribute to arenas such as education, personal development, conflict resolution, organizational consultancy, and life management. In addition, we attempt to imbue our teaching with a respectful stance to our students, with an appreciation of the many different contexts in which they find themselves and the many different strengths they already bring to the art of psychotherapy. Indeed, we suspect that collectively we may learn more from the participants in our training workshops than they from us!

In this book we attempt to provide a frame for the solution-focused model that has been helpful for us in our work and invite you, as the reader, to consider the ideas from your own context and perspective. We invite you to read the book in an experiential fashion and to try out the ideas in your own life; we encourage you to become solution detectives toward your ongoing development as therapists and discover the many clues to progress that already exist in your successful practice.

Overview of Chapters

We have attempted to structure the book chapters based on a simple formulation of the solution-focused model. Chapter 1 outlines the background to the approach and the metaphor of being a solution detective. Chapters 2 through 5 outline the model in action with a series of titles that mirror the developmental stages of the approach, notably: "Starting Where You Are At," "Where Do You Want to Go?", "How Far Have You Come?", and "What Is the Next Step?".

Finally, Chapter 6, "When Therapy Doesn't Go Well," considers some of the obstacles in applying the model and how these can be overcome.

How to Use This Book

This book is designed to give you an "experiential" sense of solution-focused therapy. It is full of practice exercises and we advise you to try these out in relation to your own professional practice. Each chapter also contains a case study that gives you an opportunity to try out the ideas in relation to a specific case. Sample answers/approaches are given at the back of the book. (These are by no means the "right" answers, and are just designed to get you started. We expect that many of your own ideas will be far more useful.)

Adapting the Practice Exercises to Working in a Small Group

The book is suitable for individual students and those studying in pairs or in small groups. Although the practice exercises are written with the individual reader in mind, most of them are best adapted to work in a small group, thus giving greater opportunity for skills practice. To do this simply consider the following procedure:

1. Each member should spend a few minutes reading through the questions in the exercise (it may be helpful to make some notes in a workbook).
2. Within the group identify a person to take the role of speaker and another to take the role of listener. The remaining group members can take on the role of observers.
3. Decide how long you want to do the exercise (five to ten minutes each way is sufficient). You should repeat the exercise a few times in the group, switching roles to ensure different people have an opportunity in different roles.

4. In the role of speaker: Speaking to the listener, talk about your answers to the questions. It may be helpful to go through them one by one, or you may prefer to follow the flow of the conversation around the theme.
5. In the role of listener: Carefully listen to your partner. Encourage him or her to keep speaking and to elaborate about the questions in the exercise. See yourself in the role of a solution-focused counselor, respectfully asking the questions and being curious and interested in the answers and valuing what the speaker says.
6. In the role of observer: Carefully listen to the process and feedback to both parties at the end; comment to the listener on the listening skills you have observed; comment to the speaker on further strengths you have observed.
7. After the agreed time for the exercise, take time to debrief and constructively offer feedback to one another before repeating the exercise in different roles.

Feedback, Please

As is our practice in our training workshops (and in our practice with clients), we very much welcome any feedback you have about the ideas contained in this book. We invite you to contact us with your comments and thoughts about what worked and didn't work for you. Please feel free to contact us at:

Brief Therapy Group
Chelmsford House
1 Chelmsford Road, Ranelagh
Dublin 6, Ireland

e-mail:
john@brieftherapy.ie
brendan@brieftherapy.ie
melissa@brieftherapy.ie

Web site:
www.brieftherapy.ie

Acknowledgments

So many people have positively contributed to the writing of this book. We are grateful to all our colleagues and mentors and the many people who have attended our training courses, from whom we have learned so much. We would specifically like to acknowledge Chris Iveson, Evan George, and Harvey Ratner of the Brief Therapy Practice in London. They have collectively been influential in teaching us the ideas of brief therapy and supportive in our development as trainers. We thank them for their spirit of generosity. We would also like to thank Scott Miller of the Institute of Therapeutic Change in Chicago who has been an inspiration to us in his continuous quest to understand the therapeutic process, and whose visits to Dublin have given singular boosts to the development of the Brief Therapy Group. Thanks also to Ben Furman, for helpful debate about the ideas behind the book, and to Imelda McCarthy for encouraging the development of our team.

We are also indebted to Eva Sharry for her Trojan efforts in putting together the original design for the book's layout and to John Johnston-Kehoe for putting the finishing touches on the manuscript. Thanks also to the members of our counseling practice, including our colleague Colman Dunne who has been supportive to this project and to Brian Gillen and Sheila Hawkins who keep the practice running smoothly with skill and humor.

A special thanks to Michael whose peaceful presence in Ferrals les Corbières encouraged us to feel relaxed and tranquil while this book was being completed.

We would also like to thank the partners from our personal lives: Geraldine, Brídín, and Tim, for their patience and support when our attention was turned toward the development of this book.

Finally, we would like to acknowledge our clients and trainees: without their insight and ideas for change this book could never have been written. We are continually honored to witness people's unique ability to create a better future.

Chapter 1

Becoming a Solution Detective

1. Always approach a case with an absolutely blank mind, which is always an advantage. Form no theories, just simply observe and draw inferences from your observations.

2. It should be your business to know things. To train yourself to see what others overlook. In an investigation, the little things are infinitely the most important.

3. Results are come by always putting yourself in the other fellow's place, and thinking what you would do yourself. It takes some imagination, but it pays.

The Art of Detection by Sherlock Holmes*

The role of a counselor or therapist can be likened to that of a great crime detective such as Sherlock Holmes. Much can be learned from his approach to the art of detection. Similar to a skilled brief therapist, he emphasizes the importance of approaching each case with a "blank mind," uncluttered by hypotheses or theories. He considers it essential to think differently, and to value significant details and little things "as infinitely the most important." In addition, as with a sensitive counselor, he knows that results depend on empathetically understanding "the other fellow"; seeing the world through their eyes.

Many writers have likened the role of a solution-focused therapist to that of a crime detective (Selekman, 1997; Van Bilsen, 1991). However, they have not chosen the wise, measured style of Sherlock Holmes as the perfect role model, but rather the peculiar, bumbling style of the famous TV detective Columbo (see Case Example 1.1). Columbo is an unassuming, dumb-appearing detective who drives an old, beat-up car and wears a shabby white raincoat, but is always suc-

---

*All quotes from Sherlock Holmes that appear throughout the text are from *The Science of Deduction and Analysis* by Sherlock Holmes (Conan Doyle, 2001).

Case Example 1.1.
Lieutenant Columbo Takes on a Suspect

"I hope I'm not intruding on your privacy, coming to your home like this," says Lieutenant Columbo, "but one thing still bothers me that I need your help with."

"That's no problem," says Grant. "I'm always happy to help the police department. Do come in. Can I make you a drink?"

"Oh, that's not necessary, sir."

"Oh, it's okay, Lieutenant, you're off duty. Join me in a Scotch. It would be my privilege."

"Okay, sir, thank you."

Grant pours two Scotches and hands one to Columbo, who takes a sip.

"Mmm, that tastes really good, sir."

"It's a twelve-year-old single malt."

"Wow, I've never had one of those before, really good. My wife, she doesn't think I should drink whiskey."

Grant smiles and says, "So Lieutenant, how can I help you?"

"Oh, sorry, sir. Let me think, I had a loose end I needed to tie up that I knew you could help me with. I have it written down here."

Columbo fumbles for a few minutes in his shabby coat and takes out his notebook, which he flicks through. Grant sighs impatiently.

"Ah, yes, here it is. The day before Barnes was killed, you told me you had lunch with him here at 1 p.m. Is that right?"

"That's right."

"Chicken salad that your wife had left out for you both, if I remember correctly," continues Columbo, reading from his notes.

"That's right, detective. You note things well, but I fail to see where this is leading."

"Well, you see, he was positively identified in a local Italian restaurant, 'Luigi's'—do you know it?"

"I've heard of it," Grant replies briskly.

"At one o'clock the same day? What puzzles me is why he would have lunch there if he knew he was coming to have lunch with you."

"Maybe he was hungry," Grant says weakly.

"Or maybe, he knew he wasn't coming here for lunch. Maybe there was another reason for him being here."

Grant becomes a little agitated as Columbo proceeds . . .

Source: This sample dialogue, which typifies Columbo's approach to detective work, is adapted from the TV series *Columbo* and novels by Harrington (1996).

cessful in solving the crime and unmasking the killer. He always adopts a polite, almost obsequious approach to each suspect. He appears bumbling and goes off into long tangents about his wife or his car to make his suspects feel at ease and to open up. He confides in them the difficulties he is having with the case and seeks their help in solving it. His trademark is to return continually to the main suspect with another question or to tie up a loose end. This peculiar bumbling, but persistent, style masks an extremely shrewd detective who is remarkably successful in getting suspects to open up and incriminate themselves.

Therapists can learn a lot from Columbo's unassuming, "one-down," seemingly nonexpert way of interviewing people. The clients are viewed as the experts and they are the ones most consulted about the case. They hold key knowledge and are encouraged to open up. Just as Columbo is always appreciative of how the suspects cooperate (letting Columbo into the house, agreeing to answer one more question), and just as he is always complimentary (as in Case Example 1.1 about his host's choice of whiskey), so the solution-focused therapist is appreciative of each example of client cooperation and always seeks to identify and value client strengths and skills.

Becoming a Solution Detective

Although Sherlock Holmes and Columbo are excellent role models for the solution-focused therapist, they are not perfect ones. There is one fundamental difference between their approach and that of a solution-focused therapist: Columbo and Sherlock Holmes are problem detectives and solution-focused therapists are solution detectives. The former are intent on investigating the crime and unmasking the killer. The latter are intent on discovering the solution and in crediting the client with this achievement.

Although Columbo's relationship with suspects is polite and deferential, it is always adversarial; his intention is to lure them into inadvertently incriminating themselves. The solution detective's relationship with clients is always collaborative and transparent, and his or her intention is to lure clients into inadvertently complimenting themselves, and recognizing their own strengths and potential.

Although Sherlock Holmes admires the prowess and intelligence of his suspects, his relationship is always competitive; his intention is to skillfully outwit and win one over on them. The solution detective also admires the client's intelligence and ability, but the relationship is interdependent and cooperative, based on client and therapist working together from their respective strengths (the client as expert on his or her life and the therapist as expert on therapeutic interviewing) to achieve a win-win outcome (a win for the client in terms of the therapeutic goal achieved and a win for the therapist in the satisfaction of another successful outcome).

Making the Shift As a Therapist

Making the shift from therapist to solution detective can be difficult, given the fact that the bulk of therapist training focuses on problem detection and the skills for being a good problem detective. Certainly, this was the authors' experience of initial psychotherapy training. We were taught the importance of looking for and analyzing problems, of skillfully pinpointing what was wrong in clients' lives, so this could be concisely summarized and sensitively fed back to them in the form of diagnosis or interpretation. Case discussions with colleagues became centered on elaborate exposés of clients' problems. The more problems we found and the more interwoven and intergenerational they were the better. A truly great therapist would quickly and concisely find out what was really going on and discover even more elaborate problems beneath the surface, some of which not even the clients themselves were aware of!

On learning solution-focused therapy, we became interested in the reverse process. What if, instead of putting all this time and effort into understanding and categorizing problems, we channeled our energies into pinpointing and understanding strengths in clients? What if we

became expert detectives of solutions rather than problems? What if, instead of skillfully framing an interpretation or diagnosis to a client, we concentrated on skillfully framing compliments that were genuine and well-timed, and inspired clients to believe in themselves and to move forward? It strikes us that a well-timed, genuine framing of a person's strengths can do more good than a well-timed, genuine framing of their problems and weaknesses. This in essence is the reformulation and reorientation on which solution-focused therapy is based.

In this book we encourage you to become solution rather than problem detectives, both toward your clients and toward your own developing practice as a therapist. We encourage you to search for clues that reveal hidden strengths and potential resources, rather than clues that demonstrate hidden problems or even more complicated pathology. We suggest you use the power of your thinking in a different direction, to generate new solutions and alternative ways forward in your work. Consider Practice Exercise 1.1 as one means to reorient yourself as a solution detective.

Practice Exercise 1.1. Identifying Your Strengths

The purpose of this exercise is to become a solution detective toward your own work as a therapist. The aim is to discover clues to your good practice and to pinpoint what is going well rather than what is going poorly, highlighting your strengths, skills, and resources.

1. Think of a piece of work you have completed as a therapist recently that you feel was successful. Use a real case if possible.
2. Ask yourself the following questions, making note of the ideas you generate:

   - What went well in the work and how do you feel about this?
   - What did you do as a therapist that helped the work go well?
   - What skills and strengths did you bring to the work that helped it to go well?
   - What do these skills reveal about you as a therapist?

Looking for Clues to the Solution

> The best place to hide anything is where everyone can see it.
>
> Sherlock Holmes

Like Sherlock Holmes, good detectives know how to look differently at the facts. They know how to free their minds from the clutter of obvious hypotheses in order to consider the data from a creative angle to reveal new clues and possibilities. They know how to evaluate and weigh the evidence and to distinguish clues which mark the solution from red herrings that lead to a dead end. In addition, the solution detective has a very particular angle on things. Whereas the problem detective looks for clues that reveal deeper problems and diagnoses, the solution detective looks for clues that reveal hidden strengths and positive possibilities. In interviewing clients the solution detective asks very different questions and the responses are filtered through very different lenses in their minds. Consider some more of the differences as listed in Table 1.1.

TABLE 1.1. Comparison of a Problem and a Solution Detective

Problem Detective	Solution Detective
Looks for "clues" that will reveal deeper problems and diagnoses.	Looks for "clues" that reveal hidden strengths and positive possibilities.
Tries to understand fixed problem patterns in clients' lives.	Tries to understand how positive change occurs in clients' lives.
Elicits detailed descriptions of problems and unwanted memories.	Elicits detailed descriptions of goals and preferred futures.
Interested in categorizing problems and applying diagnoses.	Interested in the person "beyond the problem" and in the unique story he or she has to tell.
Focuses on identifying "what's wrong," "what's not working," and on deficits in individuals, families, and communities.	Focuses on identifying "what's right and what's working," on strengths, skills, and resources in individuals, families, and communities.
Interprets and highlights times the clients "resist" or are inconsistent in their responses.	Highlights and appreciates any time the client cooperates or goes along with the therapist's questions.
Explores how trauma has affected or damaged clients.	Explores how clients have coped with trauma and how they have survived its damaging effects.

Source: Adapted from Sharry, 2001.

Thinking Strength

Perhaps the fundamental shift from being problem to solution focused is in how we think about and respond to our clients. All our questions and responses are imbued with a belief in client strengths, skills, and resources. This is not to deny that clients have problems or to minimize their impact on their lives, but rather it is out of a belief that a reorientation is more helpful. If clients do solve their problems or learn to live more resourcefully in spite of their problems, they do so as a result of their personal strengths and resources, rather than their weaknesses and deficits.

As Baruch Shalem put it: "There is nothing wrong with you that what is right with you couldn't fix" (as cited in O'Connell, 1998, p. 19). To use another example (described in Sharry, 2001), a middle-aged man may become depressed for a variety of reasons: he may have had a recent trauma or loss in his life, he may be having relationship problems with his partner, he may be reliving a childhood pattern of relating, and/or he may be obsessed about negative events in his life. How this man solves the problem of his depression may have little connection with the original causes, but will generally be due to his own strengths and resources. For example:

- he may have the strength of self-awareness to understand the causes of his depression and to distance himself from them;
- he may have the courage to draw on the support of friends and family;
- he may have the persistence to get out and to do things, such as work or engaging in leisure; or
- he may be able to coach himself and use positive self-talk to overcome negative ruminations.

The solution is ultimately due to his own actions and emerges from within his own strengths and resources. If he receives help, such as informal family support, this will be successful only insofar as he is able to make use of this support. His ability to relate to his family and draw on their support is a critical variable. Even in the case of formal help, such as counseling, it only works with his cooperation and ability to make the counseling work for him. Thus collaborating with clients' strengths and aspirations is the most likely route to success.

Framed another way, the aim of this strengths-based focus is to connect with and invoke the client's own self-healing potential. This approach mirrors that of Carl Rogers, regarded by many as the "father" of modern counseling, as he formulated the preconditions for therapeutic change:

> Gradually my experience has forced me to conclude that the individual has within himself the capacity and the tendency, latent if not evident, to move forward toward maturity. In a suitable psychological climate this tendency is released and becomes actual rather than potential. . . . Whether one calls it a growth tendency, a drive towards self-actualization, or a forward-moving directional tendency, it is the mainstream of life, and is, in the last analysis, the tendency upon which all psychotherapy depends. (Rogers, 1961, p. 35)

Though solution-focused therapy is perhaps more directional and focused than the nondirective model proposed by Rogers, the solution-focused therapist also seeks out this self-healing or self-actualizing drive, but does this by actively focusing on client strengths and resources. Hidden or potential client strengths are thus the first clues the solution detective looks for in the search for a solution. Case Study 1.1 is an example of how potential strengths can be identified from reviewing a case referral to a family clinic.

Looking for Clues with Your Own Clients

> It is of the highest importance in the art of detection to be able to recognize, out of a number of facts, which are incidental and which vital.

> Sherlock Holmes

As therapists, it can be difficult to focus on a client's strengths, particularly if we are having difficulties in working with a case, are pessimistic about the possibility of progress, or feel negative about the client. However, this is often the best time to think differently and to begin to view the client and the therapy through a strengths-based lens.

Case Study 1.1

Consider the following referral to a family clinic. Although on initial reading it can appear negative (as many referrals do), what clues to the solution are there in the description? What client strengths do you see? What questions might you ask to explore these clues and to begin to uncover the solution?

Mary is a mother of four children, ages two to ten. The visiting health nurse is concerned that the youngest child is being neglected: he is dirty and rarely attended to by his mother when she visits. Mary is very sensitive to any criticism about her parenting. She has a lot of previous involvement with professional services and the case notes suggest that Mary generally has been hostile to criticism and advice. The case notes also say that Mary was abused as a child and that she is a long-term alcoholic who has been drinking on and off for many years. Mary attends a community education course five times a week and there are concerns that the children are inadequately supervised during this time.

Write down all the possible clues you find, as well as the corresponding questions you might ask the client to explore them.

A list of possible answers is included at the back of the book. (This is not exhaustive and you will almost certainly be able to generate many more.)

The effect of such a reviewing or reframing of a case can be two-fold. First, identifying both client strengths and strengths in your therapeutic approach may provide clues to making progress. Second, your changed thinking may alter your attitude toward the client and thus the interpersonal dynamic that is occurring. Constructive thinking may cause you to be more accepting and more understanding of a client and transform a conflictual therapeutic relationship into a more collaborative alliance. Put another way, a conscious decision to change your thinking to a more strengths-based stance can help you communicate more readily two of the core attitudes which Carl Rogers deemed as essential to therapeutic progress: unconditional positive regard and empathic understanding (Rogers, 1961). Consider now applying these ideas to one of your cases in Practice Exercise 1.2.

Practice Exercise 1.2.
Looking for Clues with Your Own Clients

A. Think of a client that you have found challenging to work with currently or in the past. Now think of three positive characteristics you can attribute to this client and list them below. For example, what do you admire about your client despite the difficulties inherent in the case?

1.

2.

3.

B. Now think about three things that you did/said during your work with the client that you felt helped make the session work better. For example, what positive qualities, which you are pleased about, did you bring to the case in spite of any difficulties?

1.

2.

3.

Summary

In this chapter we have described the principles that underpin the work of a solution-focused therapist. Using the metaphor of being a solution detective, we have attempted to describe how this work is distinct from traditional psychotherapy in the clues for which the therapist and client search, notably client strengths, resources, goals, and preferred futures as opposed to client deficits, problems, and unwanted pasts. Before we consider the search for each of these clues in Chapters 3 to 6 and embark on a journey in search of the solution, let's look at a very important, although often forgotten, initial step in the next chapter—starting where the client is.

Chapter 2

Starting Where You Are At

A tourist driving through rural Ireland got lost on the small roads. Frustrated, he eventually stopped and asked a farmer how he could get back on the main road to Cork city. "Ah," said the farmer, "If I was going to Cork, I wouldn't start from here. I would start from somewhere else."

Irish Joke

As a trainee or experienced therapist reading this book, you will have your own view on solution-focused therapy (SFT). You may be an experienced practitioner interested in revisiting SFT in a different book; you may be experienced in other therapeutic models and curious as to how SFT might contribute to your practice; you may be completely new to the therapeutic field and interested in discovering more; or you may be starting from a mixture of one or more of these positions or indeed, from somewhere else entirely!

Just as SFT emphasizes respectfully joining with clients, accepting and understanding their position rather than being critical or assuming or indeed insisting they should start from somewhere else, this book encourages you to take a similar stance toward your development as a therapist. Our aim as authors is to encourage you to reflect about and understand the strengths of your practice and to invite you to consider new ideas and possibilities. You don't have to believe or accept any of the ideas in this book, or indeed do anything differently to benefit from them.

Although in its earlier formulation the principles of SFT were placed in opposition to the principles of traditional therapy (as discussed in Chapter 1), in practice the ideas have much in common and resonate with those from traditional therapies. For example, the person-centered therapy emphasis on the core therapeutic attitudes of genuineness, unconditional positive regard (or acceptance), and empathic understanding (Rogers, 1986) clearly underlie the respectful listening proposed by SFT. The behavioral therapy emphasis on concrete goals, scaling, and measurable change resonates with that of SFT (Lazarus, 1989). The importance of helping clients to think differently and more constructively is shared by the cognitive therapies (Beck, 1976; Ellis, 1998). Even psychodynamic therapy, sometimes framed in opposition to SFT, may share some common ground in that both approaches are sensitive to interpersonal and relationship factors in clients' lives (Freud, 1949).

Starting Where You Are At As a Therapist

> A man should keep his little brain-attic stocked with all the furniture that he is likely to use, and the rest he can put away in the lumber-room of his library, where he can get it if he wants it.

Sherlock Holmes

Even if you start from the viewpoint of a different model, you may still find some common ground with the ideas expressed in this book, as well as reservations and doubts. The important thing is to under-

stand and accept the mixture of beliefs, knowledge, and experiences that have brought you to this point and decide which ones you want to keep and are helpful to your practice and which you want to develop or change. As Sherlock Holmes suggests, we invite you to decide which "furniture" is best to keep in the "brain-attic" as you face a client and which is best left behind. Practice Exercise 2.1 will help you discern your viewpoint.

Starting Where the Client Is At

> Results are come by always putting yourself in the other fellow's place, and thinking what you would do yourself. It takes some imagination, but it pays.

> Sherlock Holmes

At the heart of therapy lies not a theoretical model or a set of techniques, but a human relationship. Not much can happen unless we find a way of joining with and forming a therapeutic alliance with our clients. This alliance forms the platform on which therapy is built. In

---

Practice Exercise 2.1.
Starting Where You Are At As a Therapist

Consider the following questions:

1. What beliefs and principles do you bring to your practice as a therapist? Which of these are most helpful to you? How do they help you?
2. Which therapeutic models/approaches do you apply in your work? Which of these are most helpful to you? How do they help you?
3. What personal qualities/abilities/experiences strongly influence your practice? Which of these are most helpful to you? How do they help you?
4. What feedback do you receive from clients that indicates which elements of your practice are helpful to them?
5. In developing your practice as a brief therapist, what things do you *not* want to change?
6. Of all these principles, qualities, and beliefs, which ones do you want to keep as you develop professionally?

simple terms, it is difficult to conceive of therapy being successful unless the client believes that we are on his or her side and have his or her best interests at heart. The centrality of a good therapeutic alliance is well-established across all therapies, even nonpsychological ones. It has been shown consistently in studies to be the single biggest factor that the therapist can influence in producing a positive outcome (Garfield and Bergin, 1994; Hubble, Duncan, and Miller, 1999). Although SFT is often criticized because it does not appear to emphasize the importance of joining and relationship-building skills, these are preconditions to the approach. Solution-focused techniques are reliant on the solid platform of a therapeutic alliance. To use the metaphor of the solution detective, it is important to remember that solution detection is a collaborative enterprise; the most important detective is not the therapist but the client. The client's involvement in the process is the critical variable to ensure the successful detection of a solution. For this reason we need to work hard to inspire clients to be fellow detectives and to draw them into the solution-building process. However, we need to be sensitive with regard as to where they start from and to the fact that they initially may be a problem detective rather than a solution detective. While through our genuine intentions and empathetic tailoring of our approach we can do much to entice a client on the exciting journey of solution discovery, at the end of the day, our intention is to be solution-focused and not solution-forced (Nylund and Corsiglia, 1994). It is important that we are respectful of clients' starting places, that we join with them on their own terms, and that we try to understand the world from their point of view.

Joining with Clients

So how can you as a therapist join or connect with a client? What qualities or therapeutic stance will help you establish an alliance? Although there are certain principles and guidelines, the process is mediated by the many different personal qualities and experiences that therapist and client bring to the therapeutic encounter. The relationship at the heart of the therapeutic encounter is a unique interchange between two people. The way you connect with one client may not work with another. Two different therapists are likely to connect differently with the same client and two different clients are likely to call for different styles of connecting from the same therapist. In the following we describe three principles for joining with clients: problem-free talk, the importance of listening, and joining using humor. This is not intended as a prescriptive list and what counts is that you, as a therapist, develop your own style of connecting with clients. This style should be flexible enough to meet the needs of a range of clients while matching your personality and drawing on your strengths as a person.

Problem-Free Talk

Clients often begin therapy immersed in their presenting problem (for example, depression or alcohol abuse), and it is easy for a therapist to see them simply in terms of this problem. There is a danger in connecting with a client's problem rather than with the client as a person. The starting point of SFT is to see the clients not as defined by their deficits and difficulties, but rather as persons who are more than the problem that brings them to therapy. A key way to ensure that we connect with the person is to engage in problem-free talk, especially at the start of the session. In problem-free talk the therapist is interested in getting to know the client as a person with talents, hopes, values, aspirations, interests, and hobbies.

For example, on meeting a suicidal man for the first time, the therapist does not immediately ask him about his suicide attempt or depression, but engages him in talking about the positive aspects of his life such as hobbies, work, or family concerns. On meeting a family for the first time, the therapist may spend some time talking to them about what they like to do as a family, what trips and holidays they like, and even what they like about each other. The idea of problem-free talk is that it allows us to connect with clients as people who are much more than the problem that brings them to therapy, and to note the many positive aspects of their lives which may often be overlooked and undervalued.

Even though it may resemble social chitchat, problem-free talk is a skilled process. During problem-free talk, the therapist is looking for clients' strengths and resources that may be helpful in resolving the problem. For example, a female client may share how relaxing she finds walking by the seaside and this can be suggested later as a task to help the client manage her anxiety. Fundamentally, the aim of problem-free talk is to join with clients so that an alliance can be built to facilitate the therapist and client working together to solve the problem. When we connect positively with clients and recognize the potentials and strengths they have, they can often be freed to set goals and talk about what they want to change.

Many therapies emphasize the importance of initial conversation that is not problem focused, and agree that the aim of this is to build rapport, to put clients at their ease, and to establish an alliance. This is often considered something preliminary to be done quickly before getting on to the "substance" of the therapy. In SFT, however, problem-free talk is the substance of the therapy and can occupy a large amount of time during a session.

The Importance of Listening

The importance of listening carefully to clients is perhaps the least disputed principle in counseling and therapy. This is best exemplified by the work of Carl Rogers (1961), who cited the basic human relationship between therapist and client as the crucible of change. Rogers argued that until the client felt understood and knew that the therapist had his or her best interests at heart, little therapeutic change could take place. He described in much detail the skills of what he called "empathetic listening" such as reflecting back, acknowledging, paraphrasing, and summarizing, all of which were important in creating a solid therapeutic alliance.

SFT also emphasizes the importance of listening to clients and, in many ways, the skills and techniques used can be seen as an addition to the core Rogerian counseling skills and techniques just outlined. When solution-focused therapists listen, however, they listen and acknowledge not only the pain and suffering of the client but also the client's strengths and resilience in response to the problems he or she has.

When solution-focused therapists reflect on what clients have said, the words are passed through a strengths-based filter which frames understanding in ways that open up possibilities and choices. The aim is to hold up a positive, reflective mirror to the client of his or her own abilities and strengths. Although the client may despair, the therapist continues to believe in the client and in the potential of a collaborative therapeutic alliance to move things forward. A gentle, affirming, nonimpositional, but persistent listening style characterizes this approach. Rather than listening neutrally, we are listening for the client's strengths, skills, and resources; we are listening for what's right, not just for what's wrong. Consider the following strengths-based listening to a very stressed and depressed parent.

CLIENT: Do you know it got so bad, that on Saturday I felt like running away and leaving them all, but I couldn't do it.

THERAPIST: Things got so bad for you then that you felt like leaving . . . yet you didn't. . . . What made you hang in there?

CLIENT: Well, I thought of how alone my children would be if I left, of how much they need me.

THERAPIST: Sounds like you have a lot of love for them . . . that you really want to be there for them?

CLIENT: [A little tearful] Yes.

THERAPIST: What does that say about you as a person . . . that you want to be there for your children . . . even despite the pain you feel yourself?

CLIENT: [Pause] . . . It means that I want to be the best mother I can be for them.

THERAPIST: I can really see that.

It is important not to reduce listening to a set of techniques and miss the essential interpersonal relationship that underpins the work. Rogers, in his later work, moved from a focus on techniques and skills to a focus on the counselor's attitudes toward the client and how the client perceives the relationship. He came to emphasize the essential attitudes of genuineness, unconditional positive regard (or acceptance), and empathic understanding which the therapist needs to communicate with the client (Rogers, 1961).

A strengths-based or solution-focused approach builds on Rogers's three basic attitudes of genuineness, unconditional positive regard, and empathy while adding one more: a sense of respectful curiosity toward the client. When we listen to clients, we are interested in them as people, we are curious about their goals and what they want in their lives, and we are interested in finding more about the strengths and resources they possess which will help them reach their goals. This attitude of respectful curiosity runs like a thread through all techniques of SFT. In addition, strengths-based listening expands the limited range of traditional approaches to listening. Miller, Duncan, and Hubble (1997) note:

> Unfortunately, much of what has been written about and consid-ered empathic has focused almost exclusively on the therapist's identifying and connecting with the client's negative feelings and personal experiences (e.g., clients' pain or suffering, their despair or feelings of hopelessness, their present difficulties, and the history of the complaint). However, since client strengths and resources contribute greatly to psychotherapy outcome, we would do well to adopt a broader view of empathy, a view that encompasses the light as well as the dark, the hope as well as the despair, the possibility as well as the pain. (p. 12)

Genuinely and respectfully listening to clients' hopes and aspira-tions, strengths and successes, talents and special abilities, contrib-utes to a powerful empathetic connection, and it is useful from a solu-tion-focused perspective in building the reservoir of resources with which to construct a solution.

The Importance of Problem-Focused Listening

Many novice therapists, in their desire to be solution focused, may rush ahead straight to goaling and solution-building without having first listened to or connected with their clients. They focus on tech-niques and forget the person in the room. In solution-focused therapy, listening to the client's story and allowing the client to engage in problem talk and express their feelings can be important in ensuring the client feels understood and accepted.

Sensitivity to the unique client in the room should be the central guiding principle, rather than the need to ask solution-focused ques-tions. For example, it would be insensitive to ask recently bereaved clients about times when they don't feel any grief without first hear-ing and acknowledging their pain, or it would be very inappropriate to ask parents about the times when they are not unhappy about their child's terminal illness (Lethem, 1994). Consider the following se-quence of insensitive listening from a therapist to a young woman, devastated when her boyfriend suddenly left her, announcing their re-lationship was over.

Insensitive listening:

CLIENT: [Sobbing] I can't believe he's gone. I'm so lost. I thought he loved me.

THERAPIST: Are there any times you don't feel lost?

CLIENT: No, never.

THERAPIST: When do you feel even a tiny bit less upset?

CLIENT: Not even for one moment. Not even when I'm asleep. Not that I ever sleep. Or eat.

THERAPIST: Supposing you were to feel less upset. What would that be like?

CLIENT: [Shaking her head] I dunno; I just feel so lost.

Sensitive listening:

CLIENT: [Sobbing] I can't believe he's gone. I'm so lost. I thought he loved me.

THERAPIST: You sound very upset and really hurt.

CLIENT: I am. I feel like my life is over.

THERAPIST: And it is hard at the moment for you to consider a life for yourself, without him.

CLIENT: Yeah, I can't see myself living without him.

THERAPIST: Sounds like you loved him very much.

CLIENT: I did . . . and I thought we had a good thing going.

THERAPIST: There were good times?

CLIENT: Yeah, there were loads of good times . . . before it started to go wrong last year.

THERAPIST: So it was a good relationship last year . . . before things went wrong.

CLIENT: I wanted to stay and work things out, but he didn't. He just wanted to leave.

THERAPIST: That's hard, isn't it? You want to work it out and he doesn't. You can feel so rejected.

CLIENT: Yeah.

[Later]

THERAPIST: I'm sorry that things are so difficult for you at the moment . . . and I'm wondering what your hope is for coming here?

CLIENT: I dunno; I just want him back.

THERAPIST: You're wondering if anything can be done to get the relationship back?

(Adapted from an example by Eve Lipchik, 1994)

In the first example, the therapist is rushing ahead of the distressed client to establish exceptions without having properly joined with her or establishing a goal. It would not be surprising if this client dropped out and didn't come to the next session. In the second example, the therapist sensitively tries to stay with the client and to understand her feelings and thoughts. Yet through this, the therapist is reflecting back strengths of the client ("you loved him"), exceptions ("there were good times"), and opening up possibilities ("and it is hard at the moment for you to consider a life for yourself, without him"). Crucially, the therapist takes time to allow the client to express her feelings and to build an alliance with her. Later in the session, the therapist begins to establish a goal with the client and to look at how she wants to move forward. Essentially, SFT does not replace sensitive, respectful, and accurate listening, but builds on these skills and above all stays with where the client is and with what is important to him or her.

Joining Using Humor

Laughter is the quickest distance between two people.

Boldt, 1997

Humor is probably the most common way that people connect and join with one another. Many interpersonal relationships, whether intimate or otherwise, are built upon or sustained by a shared sense of humor. Indeed it is hard to conceive of any effective human relationship that is devoid of humor. Making jokes and sharing laughter is probably a more frequent human interchange than rational argument or conversation! Despite the omnipresence of humor in human relation-

ships, it is notably absent in literature describing the therapeutic relationship. If you were only to read the literature, you would be led to believe that therapy is exclusively a serious, worthy, and weighty process, when in practice it is not always this way.

In our experience, humor is a very useful way to connect with clients and to communicate a sense of nonjudgmental understanding. A moment of shared laughter can cut through a sense of being blamed, even reduce the oppression of the problem, and crucially help build the therapeutic alliance. Of course we're not talking about any type of humor, as much humor is about belittling people and putting them down. What we're talking about is humor that builds people up, reduces hierarchy, or makes the problem look small and ridiculous.

In a child mental health setting, for example, many parents feel blamed and judged when their children have problems. In fact, this is often the greatest obstacle to forming a therapeutic alliance because it causes them to be defensive or feel oppressed. This is not helped by the fact that many mental health professionals, when they diagnose and treat childhood problems, do in fact blame parents. In the following dialogue the therapist uses humor to overcome the defensiveness of a mother who has brought her six-year-old son to a child and family clinic because of his behavioral problems. When she enters the therapist's office the child sits quietly while his mother talks at length about the problems.

MOTHER: He's really a demon at home; he throws tantrums all the time and never does what I ask. [She looks at child sitting quietly.] Of course he is making a fool of me here, sitting so quietly, good as gold.

THERAPIST: Would you believe that this often happens here.

MOTHER: What?

THERAPIST: When parents bring their children here, they often behave *very* well in my office, even though their parents are coping with really bad behavior at home.

MOTHER: [Interested] Really?

THERAPIST: And to be honest, I'm glad that your child is behaving well in my office. [Pauses and then adds self-mockingly] I really don't think I could cope if he threw a tantrum.

MOTHER: [Laughs] You'd find it hard to cope too.

THERAPIST: Absolutely!

The therapist's humorous response indirectly communicated to the mother that the therapist understood how difficult it was to manage tantrums and to feel incompetent in the face of them. This helps break the mother's sense of being judged and creates an alliance that helps her let go of engaging in problem-talk (to make sure the therapist understood how bad things could be) and move to consider solutions with the therapist on her side.

Probably the reason that humor is not often cited as a way of connecting in the psychotherapy literature is because humor can be risky. It can be taken the wrong way or add to a sense of misunderstanding, but perhaps no more so than other mistimed or overused joining techniques (for example, it is inappropriate to suddenly engage in prob-

---

Practice Exercise 2.2.
Finding Your Way of Joining with Clients

1. Think of someone (outside your family) who helped you solve something important in your life. The person could be a therapist, teacher, colleague, or someone else. What made you trust that person? What did this person do and say that made you feel that he or she could help you and was on your side?
2. Think of a time, when working as a therapist, that you were able to connect with/empathetically understand a client. What did you do and say that made this possible?
3. What do you think your style of joining with/connecting with clients is? What personal qualities do you have that helps you do this?

lem-free talk when a client has just revealed that he or she was sexually abused as a child). What is essential is to use humor in a sensitive, skilled way that builds people up and helps communicate that you understand their predicament and are on their side.

Taking Time to Join with Clients

Sometimes establishing a therapeutic alliance or joining with clients is easy and takes so little time that it is unnoticed as a stage in therapy. Yet on other occasions it proves to be difficult and takes more time and consideration. Many therapies run into trouble when the therapist rushes ahead of the client without having first established the platform of a therapeutic alliance. The therapist rushes to use techniques without having first sufficiently understood, and without having sufficiently joined with the client. In these cases, the therapist will invariably have to return to the beginning and listen first.

Case Study 2.1

Consider the following client who presents to a private practice for counseling. He has self-referred, so you have no prior knowledge about the client or the case, except what he shares with you during the first session. After reading the description of the case, take time to write down some ideas you might have concerning how to work with the client in a respectful way.

Max is a young man in his twenties who is coming to therapy to overcome sexual abuse from his childhood. In the first session he talks about his current life being unfulfilling: he is disappointed that he has not been able to make any romantic connections in his life, although this is something he would really like to develop. He is unclear how coming to therapy will help, but was encouraged by a close friend who he has great trust in. He looks to you for answers and guidance on how to resolve his current dilemmas, as he has found the past few years a struggle.

Consider the chapter you have just finished reading and the balance between listening constructively to the client's story and being able to respectfully use a "solution filter." After you have finished, you can refer to the back of the book for some of our ideas and suggestions regarding the case.

Eve Lipchik (1994), one of the originators of the model, criticizes the "rush to be brief" and argues that good solution-focused therapy depends as much on empathic listening and relationship-building skills as any other therapy. So remember in your practice, don't be afraid to "go slow" and to take time to connect with and understand your clients.

Summary

The establishment of a successful therapeutic alliance can be seen as the foundation upon which further progress in therapy rests. Discovering ways to connect with the client in an empathic person-to-person relationship prepares the ground for further constructive collaboration. In reading this chapter we hope that you have had time to reflect on and appreciate your own unique way of connecting and establishing alliances with your clients. However, as the research indicates (Hubble, Duncan, and Miller, 1999), progress in therapy depends not just on a strong therapeutic alliance but also on the identification of what the clients want to achieve as a result of coming to therapy, that is, how they want their lives to be different. This is the subject of the next chapter.

Chapter 3

Where Do You Want to Go?

"Would you tell me please which way I ought to walk from here?" asked Alice.

"That depends a good deal on where you want to get to," said the Cat.

"I don't much care where," said Alice.

"Then it doesn't matter which way you walk," said the Cat.

"So long as I get somewhere," Alice added as an explanation.

"Oh, you're sure to do that," said the Cat, "if you only walk long enough."

Alice's Adventures in Wonderland
Lewis Carroll, 1992

Clients who present for therapy may experience a sense of being lost and disoriented in their lives, similar to what Alice experiences in the woods. They too want to "get somewhere" but are unsure about where they want to go. Assuring clients that if they persist on the therapy journey they are bound to get somewhere is not necessarily the most helpful response to their difficult circumstances.

Indeed, Alice's frustrations with the Cheshire Cat give us some insight into clients' unclear feelings about where they want to go in their lives and their search for direction. It is not surprising, therefore, that the establishment of clear, agreed-upon client goals is necessary to sustain and strengthen the therapeutic alliance, while facilitating positive constructive progress in therapy.

As the Cheshire Cat reminds Alice, it is one thing to not want to be where you are but quite another to know where you want to be instead. The skilled solution detective recognizes that progress in therapy depends upon helping clients establish in clear, identifiable ways how it is they want their lives to be different (Garfield and Bergin,

1994). This process, referred to as goaling or goal setting, is the important next step in our ongoing detective story.

Before we consider how the solution detective goes about discovering clients' goals, it is useful to reflect on our own personal and professional lives and discover what goals are important to us. As with Alice, all of us, whether experienced or trainee therapists, are on a journey of discovery and face professional and personal challenges in our lives that we want to "get somewhere" with. We may have dreams or aspirations as therapists and ideas about where we want to go in our professional lives. However, getting to our destinations involves development of these dreams or aspirations into clear ideas of where we want to end up. The quickest way to complete a journey is to begin with a clear idea of where we want to go, rather than focusing on where we've been or where we don't want to go.

Practice Exercise 3.1 provides an experiential sense of the power of goal setting, as you consider where you want to go in your professional development as a therapist.

Where Do Your Clients Want to Go?

Many research studies suggest that the establishment of clear, client-centered goals early in the therapy process is critical to ensur-

---

Practice Exercise 3.1. Where Do You Want to Go from Here?

1. What are your hopes and dreams as a therapist?

   How will you know you have achieved them?
   What will you be seeing, feeling, or doing differently?
   How will other people in your life know you have achieved them?

2. What goals are necessary to achieve those dreams?

   How can reading this book contribute to achieving these goals?

3. In developing your practice as a brief therapist, what things do you want to change?

   How will you know you have achieved these changes?
   What will you be seeing, feeling, and doing differently?

Source: Adapted from Furman and Ahola (1997).

ing effective outcome and is a necessary part of developing and maintaining the therapeutic alliance (Garfield and Bergin, 1994; Hubble, Duncan, and Miller, 1999). Indeed, an emphasis on goaling is often seen as a defining characteristic of brief therapy approaches and is regarded by brief therapy practitioners as a key factor in contributing to the brief (short-term) focus of the work (Walter and Peller, 2000). As the Cheshire Cat remarks, you're sure to get somewhere "if you only walk long enough" but knowing where you want to go may shorten the journey considerably.

The solution detective is very curious to identify what his or her clients want to achieve as a result of coming to therapy, i.e., in what way they want their lives to be different. As with all good detectives, solution detectives discover this information by asking clients a series of questions. These questions are designed to help the clients describe in detail their desired outcome from the therapy process. In the following, we identify two classes of questions that solution detectives use to facilitate the identification of clear, detailed, and achievable client-centered goals: outcome questions and hypothetical solution questions.

Although experienced therapists may have their own versions of these questions, trainee therapists may find some useful ideas here on how to engage clients in the goaling process. Our aim is to offer you a menu of possibilities for negotiating clear, focused, client-centered goals from the outset.

Outcome Questions: What Do You Want from the Therapy?

Clients may have many different problems in their lives and many different associated goals and ambitions, all of which are subject to change and flux. When clients decide to seek help, they bring some or all of these problems and goals into the therapy room. Brief therapy is only possible, and only likely to be successful, if a focused goal is negotiated for its duration. This means that therapist and client need to negotiate which problem they are going to work on for the duration of the therapy and agree on a realistic goal for their meetings. Skilled solution detectives quickly become more focused in their questions, moving from "What would the client like to achieve in his or her life?" to "What would they like to achieve by coming to these sessions?" There are many variations on outcome questions. For example:

- What are your best hopes for coming to these meetings?
- What would be the most helpful issue to talk about today?
- What needs to happen to make these meetings helpful to you?

Future-oriented outcome questions can more creatively elicit the same information:

- How will you know that you no longer need to come to therapy?

For clients referred by others, it might be useful to inquire about their expectations.

- How will your referrer/agency know today's session has been helpful to you?
- What are your partner's best hopes for these meetings?

The thrust of all these questions is to negotiate a realistic, focused goal for therapy. They encourage clients to describe what they want in their lives, in relation to coming to therapy (goaling), as opposed to elaborating what it is they do not want (complaining). This is the first essential step of brief therapy. However, this process is by no means easy and can be particularly challenging for clients who are quite problem focused in their thinking and demoralized from previous attempts to resolve their difficulties. In fact, many clients who present for therapy have experienced, often for a considerable period of time, the frustration of repeated unsuccessful attempts to resolve their problems prior to coming to therapy.

This phenomenon, referred to as "doing more of the same that isn't working," was first commented on by the Mental Research Institute (MRI) team (Watzlawick, Weakland, and Fisch, 1974). It accounts for many clients' reluctance to engage in envisioning a life without their problems, either because they are too demoralized to do so or anxious to avoid the painful disappointment of another failed attempt at resolving their difficulties. Consequently, they may lapse into detailed descriptions of the presenting problem, hoping that the therapist can somehow directly intervene to solve it.

Given the distress that many clients present with when initially coming to therapy, it is not surprising that all of us as therapists have at times felt the urge to step in and engage in problem-solving strategies with our clients, trying to tackle the presenting problems one by one. However, in our experience, it is more effective to invite the client to imagine a future time without the problem (a hypothetical solution) and then to work backward, making a bridge from the solution to the client's current situation, rather than the other way around.

Hypothetical Solution Questions: What Will Life Be Like Without the Problem?

Hypothetical solution questions encourage the client to describe what his or her life would be like when the problems that have brought him or her to therapy have been resolved. Examples of these types of questions include:

- Suppose that our work here is successful. What will be different in your life that will tell you that treatment has been successful?

Or more elaborately,

- Imagine yourself a year from now, after you and I have worked together and successfully resolved the problem(s) that brought you here. What will be different then that will tell you the problem has been solved?

Since the beginnings of therapy, skillful therapists have been aware of the value of hypothetical solution questions and each has developed their own particular version. Perhaps the earliest example of this type of question is Ansbacher and Ansbacher's (1998) "Magic Wand" question.

- If I had a magic wand or a magic pill that would eliminate your symptom immediately, what would be different in your life?

Later therapists, such as Milton Erickson, developed their own version of the hypothetical solution question. Erickson and Rossi's (1980) "Crystal Ball" technique incorporates hypnotherapy elements that encourage clients to envision a time in the future when they are free of the presenting problem. In more recent years, de Shazer and his team's development of the "miracle question" (Berg, 1991; de Shazer, 1988) has introduced hypothetical solution questions to a wider audience of therapists. The miracle question is a key goal-setting question in SFT. It can be posed simply as:

- If the problem disappeared overnight, by magic, what would your next day be like?

Or more dramatically:

- Imagine that when you go home tonight a miracle takes place and the problem that brought you to therapy completely disappears. But of course, being a miracle, you don't know it has happened. What will be the first thing you notice the next day that will tell you it has happened?

For solution detectives, asking the miracle question is one of the most effective means of engaging clients in richly describing what their lives would be like without their problems. By posing the question in terms of a miracle, clients do not have to concern themselves with how the goal will be achieved. Instead, all they have to consider is how their lives will be different when the miracle occurs. This removes the client's anxiety that they will be somehow obliged to produce the solution and facilitates a more expansive, detailed description of the preferred solution.

THERAPIST: Imagine that when you go home tonight a miracle takes place and the problem that brought you here today disappears. You don't know it's happened because you're asleep. What will be the first thing you notice tomorrow that tells you it has happened?

CLIENT: Hum . . . I guess I'd be back to work and maybe be promoted.

THERAPIST: OK . . . but what about in the morning when you wake up? What would be the first thing you notice that would say to you that this miracle had happened?

CLIENT: I guess I would be out of bed before noon; I've been sleeping all day recently, and not bothering to get up or shower.

THERAPIST: I see, so being up and showered in the morning would be the first sign of a real difference for you. Anything else you'd notice?

CLIENT: I would get out of the house in the morning, even just to go up to the shops to get milk.

THERAPIST: Who do you think would be the first person that would notice that things were changing for you?

CLIENT: I know this sounds silly, but my dog would; I haven't been walking him in ages.

THERAPIST: So you would be up and showered before noon, perhaps having gone out to the shops and your dog would even have gotten a walk. If these things happened how would that make the rest of the day different?

Identifying and clarifying goals with clients is by no means a straightforward process and can take a substantial amount of time. Indeed, the initial standard client reply to goal-focused questions is "I don't know." In our experience, what the client often means is that he or she doesn't know at this point in time. Given a few moments to think about the question, they can come up with answers. Consequently, we often ask clients to think about the question for a few moments or guess what they think their answers might be.

When they do come up with answers, their descriptions of goals are often unclear or lacking detail. In many cases clients are quite clear about what they don't want but unsure about what they do want. It is not surprising that the process of therapy has been described as two people talking to each other trying to find out "what the hell one of them wants." In Practice Exercise 3.2, we consider how developing

Practice Exercise 3.2. Developing a Motto

Think about a goal you are working on (for example, your hopes and dreams for your future practice as a therapist).

Now take some time to think about a motto that empowers you to pursue this goal. It is important to find a motto that is unique to you, that is empowering and positive toward the goal you want to achieve. Take some time to visualize yourself in the future doing the things you want in your life. What would you say to yourself to encourage achievement of this goal?

Now write down this motto in a special way. This may involve using paints, markers, and colors. Be creative! Once you have created your special motto, keep it in a place where you can refer to it when you need encouragement and a reminder of your hopes and dreams for the future.

Source: Adapted from Furman and Ahola (1997).

a motto or slogan can be useful in helping a person develop a clear and motivating picture of a particular goal.

Developing a Detailed Description of Goals

In an investigation, the little things are infinitely the most important. Never trust to general impressions, but concentrate yourself upon details.

Sherlock Holmes

Like all good detectives, solution detectives recognize the importance of details. After asking an outcome or miracle question they take the time to ask further questions, thereby encouraging their clients to describe their goals in rich detail. This ensures that goaling is an effective contribution to the therapeutic process. There are a number of criteria that must be followed to ensure that clients' goals are described as fully as possible.

In general, goals should be

- positive and clear;
- detailed and meaningful; and
- manageable and realistic.

Positive and Clear

By positive, we mean that goals should describe the presence of something that clients want in their life as opposed to describing the absence of something undesirable. Clients understandably present to therapy with a focus on the problems they are experiencing and often assume that their role is to identify and describe these problems and deficiencies to the therapist. The main clue in the following Sherlock Holmes story (Case Example 3.1) was discovered by identifying what was missing rather than what was present on the night of the crime. Similarly, the solution detective aims to direct clients' attention to what is missing in their lives that they want, instead of focusing on the problems that are present in their lives that they don't want.

Case Example 3.1. The Dogs Didn't Bark

In the Sherlock Holmes story, "Silver Mane," a prize racehorse was stolen from its stable. When other detectives failed to solve the mystery, Holmes was called in by the insurance company to investigate. The genius he brought to the case was not only to consider what things were present on the night the horse was stolen but also what things were missing. A crucial fact was that, while many witnesses heard footsteps heading toward the stable, none heard the dogs bark. This led Sherlock Holmes to deduce that the thief was known to the dogs and ultimately to discover that it was the owner.

In therapy, the skill of the solution detective is to notice not only the problems that exist in your clients' lives, but also the things that are missing. The genius is in noticing what could be or might be in your clients' lives and thus discover new possibilities and potentials. As Sherlock Holmes might ask: "What is absent in your clients' lives that they haven't noticed is missing?"

Consider the following dialogue, which also illustrates this point.

THERAPIST: Steve, what needs to happen today for you to feel that coming here was useful?

STEVE: [Pause] I guess I don't want to feel depressed anymore. I've been feeling so down recently and I'm not sure why; I can't figure it out.

THERAPIST: So recently it has been pretty difficult. And this feeling of depression . . . what would you like to feel instead?

STEVE: I'd like to get rid of the depression. I'd like to feel happier.

The therapist in this example gently refocuses the client from talking about his depression to what he would rather be feeling. The simple use of the word "instead" can dramatically turn the conversation away from what the client does not want, to the development of what the client would like in their life. This simple shift from a negative to a positive focus can be a powerful tool in developing a clear goal with a client.

Detailed and Meaningful

The more detailed and elaborate clients' goals are, the more personal and meaningful they become. A detailed picture of the goal is much more motivating to clients and they are likely to work harder to achieve it. In addition, this clear picture of what they are striving for is more likely to inspire and lift them out of their problem. Once a positive goal has been established, the therapist becomes interested in eliciting rich detail. Consider the following dialogue, a continuation of the previous example.

THERAPIST: Steve, what would give you a sign that you were feeling lighter?

STEVE: I guess if I was eating again and sleeping; I've been having broken sleep for weeks now, which does not help.

THERAPIST: No, it does not sound like it helps. But if you began to get back into your regular pattern of eating and sleeping, that might give you a sense that things were getting better. Are there other things that would give you the sense that you were getting back to yourself?

STEVE: [Pause] I suppose if I went out with the guys after work on Friday for a drink . . . I used to meet up with them every week. Since I've been down I haven't gone out at all. They still call, though.

THERAPIST: So they would notice too, that you were getting back to the old you. Would they notice any other changes in you?

STEVE: I'd be more relaxed at work, not biting the heads off people, just having a relaxed attitude.

Notice how the therapist is successful in getting a lot of rich detail about the solution that the client seeks (e.g., eating and sleeping regularly, going out on Friday nights, and being more relaxed at work). The richer the detail the better. The therapist should ask as many follow-up questions as possible to enrich the description of this solution. Questions that encourage the sharing of this detail include:

• What do you notice that's different about yourself?
• What do you see/hear/feel differently?
• What are other people that you meet saying/doing differently?
• What do they notice that is different about you?

The following question is helpful in gathering details of the miracle goal.

• If we were to follow you for a day with a video camera after the miracle had happened, what would we record?

Notice the use of the present tense in these questions. This helps to link these envisioned activities to the present and creates an expectation of change. For many clients, the effect of describing their preferred solutions in detail can be quite dramatic. It may represent a complete reorientation from problem-focused descriptions of their life to a vision of life without the problem. This possibility can be highly motivating for clients and may help spur them into action. Equally, when preferred futures are richly described, clients may see examples of solutions already occurring in their lives, or identify small manageable steps they can take. Consider this example, taken from a family session with a mother and her teenage son.

MOTHER: He's just so lazy; he does nothing for me. He just sits around the house all day.
SON: [Listening, just closes down]
THERAPIST: What way would you like him to be in the house?
MOTHER: I'd like him to be more considerate in the house.
THERAPIST: How would you know if he was more considerate?

MOTHER: I dunno . . .

THERAPIST: [To son] Do you know what your Mom means when she says she wants you to be more considerate?

SON: [Shrugs]

MOTHER: If he just helped me a little more in the house.

THERAPIST: What way would you like him to help you in the house?

MOTHER: I don't want him to do much . . . even if he didn't get in the way when I'm working.

THERAPIST: So what would tell you that he was not in the way and was considerate?

MOTHER: [Thinks] Well, if, when I'm vacuum cleaning in the living room, he'd lift his feet when he's on the sofa . . .

SON: [Smiles]

THERAPIST: So he'd show you consideration by lifting his feet to allow you to pass with the vacuum cleaner . . . that would be a good sign. [Pause]

THERAPIST: [To son] What do you think of that? You think you could do it?

SON: Yeah, of course.

In this example, although it takes time, the therapist eventually elicits a concrete, meaningful example of what consideration means to the mother: for her son to lift his feet when she vacuums the living room. By getting to such an elaboration, we have arrived at a goal which means a great deal for the client and which is small enough to be achieved immediately. In addition, the detail has a lighthearted note, which eases the tension caused by the problem.

Manageable and Realistic

Clearly, impossible goals, improbable goals, or goals that require other people to change can appear to be significant roadblocks to client progress. However, the persistent solution detective, when confronted with these obstacles, can circumvent them in a number of ways. One of the most useful is to help clients identify whether their goals are ends in themselves or are means toward an end (Miller, 1998). For example, a client may wish to lose weight even when he or she has been diagnosed with an eating disorder. With some patient curiosity, the therapist might be able to uncover the deeper goal underlying the client's desire, such as feeling more confident or attractive. Losing weight may be only one possible means of achieving this goal. Consider the following dialogue with a student who is attending therapy to resolve an eating disorder.

SCHOOL COUNSELOR: How did you hope I might be helpful to you today?

STUDENT: I'd like my mom off my back; she is giving me such hassle.

SCHOOL COUNSELOR: What do you think it would take to get her off your back?

STUDENT: [Pause] I guess she wants me to put on weight; she is always at me to eat more.

SCHOOL COUNSELOR: Is this something you would like too?

STUDENT: No, I would like to lose more weight; I think I'm too heavy.

SCHOOL COUNSELOR: How would losing more weight be good for you?

STUDENT: [Pause] I'd feel more confident about myself and with other girls. I really feel awkward when I'm around the girls in class.

SCHOOL COUNSELOR: So you would like to feel more confident in yourself, particularly when with the other girls in the class.

Notice how the counselor gently reveals the deeper goal which underlies the student's desire to lose weight. In doing so, the counselor gently challenges the student's assumption that there is only one means to the end she desires. In practice, there are often multiple means to the same end. The emphasis in goaling is on describing what will be different, i.e., the end, rather than how it may be achieved, i.e., the means. Clarifying what are means and what are ends, and discovering more than one means to the same end are useful ways of addressing the challenge of impossible or improbable goals. In this dialogue the school counselor begins to create a new goal with the student: to be more confident in herself. From here the counselor can begin to explore other ways the student might be able to gain confidence that does not risk her health due to increased weight loss.

The question of whether goals are means or ends also arises when clients come to therapy wanting other people in their lives to change, or wanting suggestions on how to change other people. Again, clarifying the end goal that the client wants is useful. Consider the following example:

THERAPIST: If they changed how would that be helpful for you?

CLIENT: I'd be much happier.

THERAPIST: What other ways can you be happy even when they stay the same?

These questions help the client clarify what the end for him or her is if the other person changes and also seek to identify what other means are available to the same ends.

Practice Exercise 3.3. Letter from the Future

Think about a particular "big goal" you have for your life over the next five or ten years. Where would you like to be with regard to this goal?

Now take the time to write a letter from yourself five years in the future; a successful future self. Address the letter to you now. Tell yourself about your goals, accomplishments, and successes. Let yourself know the path that your future self used to achieve these goals. In the future letter you should give encouragement about the progress you have made and the benefits of all the hard work you have put into your development.

Be sure to use encouragement and hope in your description of the journey. The journey may describe hard times or difficult things that had to be addressed to ensure success. Your future self should encourage you to persist through difficult times and describe in detail the benefits of reaching your goals.

Source: Adapted from Capaccione (1979).

Finding the Solution in the Present

The grand thing is to be able to reason backwards . . . but people do not practice it much. There are a few people, however, who, if you told them a result, would be able to evolve from their own inner consciousness what the steps were which led up to that result. This power is what I mean when I talk of reasoning backwards.

Sherlock Holmes

Similar to the skills described by Sherlock Holmes, solution-building (as opposed to problem solving) involves being able to reason backward. Once the hypothetical solution is generated and the preferred future is envisioned in rich detail, the task then becomes to establish a pathway backward to the client's current situation. The most powerful way to do this (which will be explored in greater detail in Chapter 4) is to find the seeds of the solution in the present. Possible questions to probe this topic include:

- Which parts of the solution do you think sometimes exist in your life already?
- When were you closest to the solution happening?
- What would be the first sign that the solution was happening?

These questions provide a crucial link between the hypothetical solution described by the client and tangible examples of it in his or her everyday experience. In this way a "therapeutic bridge" is created between the client's current problem and the hypothetical solution (e.g., the miracle), and the client sees real possibilities for change in the direction of the preferred solution. This process of change can then be broken down into smaller, more manageable steps.

Identifying small, manageable steps is also important when the focus of therapy is not about helping the client work toward a specific goal, but supporting him or her as they work through a process of change, for example, coming to terms with loss or grief. It is particularly important in these situations to go at the client's pace. Goaling in

TAKING THERAPY STEP BY STEP MEANS LESS CHANCE OF PUTTING YOUR FOOT IN IT!

this case is intended to help the client identify signs of progress rather than a complete solution. Questions which facilitate this identification include:

- What will be the first signs to you that you are making progress?
- How will you know when you are starting to come to terms with what has happened?
- What will be the smallest sign that progress is happening?

The focus is on helping the client make the desired outcome more identifiable and achievable by describing small specific steps that are attainable. Case Study 3.1 asks you to consider how you might develop workable goals with clients to address the presented problems.

Case Study 3.1

Take time to review each case and the initial dialogue between the therapist and the client. How would you respond to the client to encourage him or her to move toward formulating goals that are useful and realistic, while respecting his or her hope for the future?

After each dialogue write down the types of question that you would use to guide the client toward a workable goal. Take time to reflect on this chapter and the various points that are outlined to help develop useful goals.

When you are finished, why not compare your answers with those of the authors at the back of the book? These are just helpful suggestions. The idea is to find your own style of working with clients to develop clear visions of the future.

Example A

Rick is a forty-year-old man who is attending counseling for the first time. His parole officer suggested he attend because of his anger outbursts and violent behavior.

THERAPIST: Rick, welcome! What are your best hopes for coming here?
RICK: [Shrugging his shoulders] Don't know.
THERAPIST: I understand that it was your parole officer's idea for you to come. Is that right?
RICK: Yes, he suggested that I should come.

(continued)

(continued)

How would you follow this initial dialogue with Rick? Write down several possibilities before you check with the back of the book. All the ideas may be useable!

Example B

Sally is a sixteen-year-old girl. She recently experienced a physical assault when someone stole her bag at a bus stop. Her mother has arranged for her to talk things through with someone.

THERAPIST: How do you think I might be able to help you here today?

SALLY: [Tearful] I just don't know. I'm so upset, everything is crashing down around me and . . . [more tears].

THERAPIST: [Handing a tissue to Sally] Sounds like things have been pretty tough for you lately.

SALLY: My life was going fine. I was hanging out, studying, my friends, boyfriend. I was great. Then it all changed last week, after the attack. I'm just staying in and not doing anything now. I can't do anything.

THERAPIST: So your life was going really well and now you feel things have stopped, for the moment?

SALLY: Yeah, I'm just very scared now . . . and angry that this happened to me.

THERAPIST: Sounds hard.

SALLY: Yeah, I just don't want to be scared anymore, scared of not leaving the house or of who might be out there.

How would you respond to Sally? Develop several possible responses that could help her to develop a goal for the sessions.

Summary

Uncovering what clients want in the form of detailed, meaningful, and concrete goals is the basis of successful brief therapy. It can develop the therapeutic alliance, as it ensures you are explicitly working together on the same goal; it can refocus the client on the solution and tap into his or her reservoir of motivation and resources; it can also keep the process focused, ensuring it lasts no longer than it needs to. In Chapter 4 we look in more detail at the clues the solution leaves in the present and the past, as it is important to appreciate just how far the client has already come.

Chapter 4

How Far Have You Come?

"I'm a very bad wizard, I must admit," said Oz.

"Can't you give me any brains?" asked the Scarecrow.

"You don't need them. You are learning something every day."

"But how about my courage?" asked the Lion anxiously.

"You have plenty of courage, I am sure," answered Oz. "All you need is confidence in yourself. There is no living thing that is not afraid when it faces danger. True courage is in facing danger when you are afraid and that kind of courage you have in plenty."

The Wizard of Oz (Baum, 1998)

Going to see a psychotherapist can be like going to see the Wizard of Oz. Although there can be great expectation and belief in the power of the wizard, the reality is that therapeutic success rests on the client's efforts. Good brief therapists realize that they are "very bad wizards" and instead believe in the wizardry of their clients who have already come so far and achieved so much.

As the Wizard of Oz points out to the Lion, he has already shown great courage in overcoming the many obstacles and dangers on his journey. Good brief therapists also value and appreciate the many ways their clients have already managed (and even solved in the past) the problem that brings them to therapy. It is these steps that clients have already taken (albeit unnoticed, undervalued, or unappreciated) toward the solution that are the subject of this chapter. Simply put, good brief therapists are interested in appreciating just how far their clients have already come.

Learning from the Past

The emphasis of the solution-focused model is clearly future focused. The aim is to encourage people to envision and imagine the futures they want and to begin to work toward these preferred futures starting from where they are. Once a goal is agreed upon, therapy becomes focused on making progress. In collaboration with the client, the solution detective searches for resources and strategies to move forward.

However, good solution detectives do not try to invent ways of making progress; they realize that clients are likely to have already made substantial progress toward their goals and may already have many resources and strategies at their disposal. Good solution detectives search for these clues that lie in the present and the past. The preferred future that a client seeks leaves its mark on the present and past. Just as many problem detectives search in a client's childhood (or even farther back to their parents' childhoods) to trace the history of a pathology or to look for a cause of the problem, so a solution detective searches the client's past to trace the development of the solution and to discover early evidence of its existence.

The past is not seen as the source of the problem, but rather as a potential resource, full of learning experiences and helpful knowledge. The past is mined for the ore of the solution rather than the detritus of the problem, or to use another metaphor, the past is harvested for its fruits rather than its weeds. Reviewing past experiences in this way can change what is discovered within. As Furman and Ahola (1992) state:

> The belief that the tragedies of the past can cause later problems and render people vulnerable to future strain can become a self-fulfilling prophecy. Conversely to think of one's past as a resource may help people in achieving their goals. . . . The opposite view that past ordeals are valuable learning experiences is equally sensible. (pp. 21, 23)

It is through this lens that solution-focused therapists view the past in order to find the building blocks to create a meaningful future.

Finding Exceptions

Problem detectives are interested in problem patterns. In their efforts to solve the problem, they seek detailed information about the

> ### Practice Exercise 4.1.
> ### Tracing the History of Your Strengths As a Therapist
>
> Consider your experience as a therapist (or in a helping relationship).
> Make a list of the skills and knowledge that you find helpful.
> When did you first learn these skills?
> When did you first notice them in your practice?
> When did you first notice these skills in your personal life?
> Who was helpful to you in developing these skills?
> Who did you learn them from (in your therapy training and before)?

events that lead up to and surround the times the problem occurs. They want to know as much as possible about all the involved parties, as well as any witnesses to the episode. They want to understand each person's account of events and to gain insight into their thoughts and feelings on what happened. Their aim is to discover each person's motivation in regards to the problem and to ultimately attribute blame to single or multiple parties.

Solution detectives, however, are interested in solution patterns. They seek detailed information on the events that lead up to and surround the times the crimes do not occur in the belief that this will reveal clues to a solution. In solution-focused therapy, these clues are framed as exceptions (de Shazer, 1985, 1988) and in narrative therapy they are framed as "unique outcomes" (White and Epston, 1990). It is believed that problem patterns are never rigidly fixed through time and different situations. There are always times and situations when the problem occurs slightly less frequently or even not at all. Indeed, the fact that a person is aware that there is a problem suggests that he or she is making a comparison to another time or situation when the problem did not exist. For example, a man who feels depressed only knows he feels this if he had other times when he was happier.

For problem detectives, these exceptions are often forgotten, ignored, or considered to be flukes. Solution-focused therapy, however, believes that it is exceptions that deserve the closest attention. They signify examples of "micro-solutions" already occurring within clients' experience and ways in which clients have been successful. They can be conceived of as clues that signal how progress can be

made. If understood and explored they can be amplified and repeated, ultimately leading to the eventual elimination of the problem and attainment of a solution.

Exceptions can occur on an ongoing basis. For example, a father may notice that late at night, when his teenage son is going to bed, they are able to have a civil conversation together rather than the usual rows that occur throughout the day. Another client may notice that she wakes more full of energy in the middle of the week when she looks forward to a special class.

Exceptions may also refer to times in the past when a client was more successful. For example, a client may recall that two years ago when she was working in a different job her life was more balanced and she was less depressed. A client may also recall happy times in her childhood when she did feel cared for by her parents. Once identified, the solution detective attempts to expand on and understand these exceptions with questions such as:

- What do you feel/think/do differently during these times?
- What do other people notice about you during these times?
- What do you notice about other people?
- What else do you notice?
- How do you make these times happen?
- What would you have to do/say to make this happen more often?
- What else would help it happen?

Consider the following example of a past exception within a marriage being explored.

HUSBAND: I'm sick of all the rows we have. It never seems to end; over and over we are fighting. I just can't put up with it anymore.

THERAPIST: Seems like the marriage has been pretty tough to stay in recently—very difficult. Tell me, has it always been as difficult, as tough to stay in the marriage? For example, what about when you first got together?

HUSBAND: God, that seems so long ago now, before the kids and the fights. [Pause] When we first got together it was great. We really got on; we were in love. I guess that is why we got married.

THERAPIST: Really? Can you think about how it was different back then?

HUSBAND: [Long pause] Well, I guess we made time for each other. Kate, my wife, she was the number one thing. I could not wait to get home from work then, because I knew we were going to do things together. We used to have great fun and just get in the car and drive off to the beach and go for long walks and talks. It was great just being together.

THERAPIST: Is that one of the differences between then and now? Having time together, just the two of you to relax and talk?

HUSBAND: I suppose. I never really thought about it but you're right. We used to spend time just enjoying each other, and now we are never together. . . . Work, kids, housework, it all seems to come first. I can't remember how long it has been since we had a conversation that was not about something to do with the kids or house.

THERAPIST: Do you think if you had some time alone together, just to relax and talk about things other than work, kids, house, would that make a difference?

HUSBAND: God, I don't know. It would be strange to try to find something to talk about again, but I suppose it would be worth it, to talk and not fight about who is doing what around the house.

This case illustrates that most problems have times, in the past or present, when the problems did not exist or were managed to a greater degree. Notice that the therapist acknowledges the hardship the husband expresses about his marriage yet gently turns the focus to find out about when the couple first met to discover if there were exceptions to the never-ending fights. The husband is able to reflect on the history of his relationship and even able to pinpoint that time together with his wife, relaxing and talking, was helpful in their remaining close. It is this past exception that can be used as a building block to future changes. Once an exception has been identified, it can be helpful to find out during subsequent sessions whether the exception has occurred again or whether clients have been successful in attempts to repeat it. For example, if the husband returns for a future session, the conversation might proceed as follows.

THERAPIST: What has been helpful since last time we met?

HUSBAND: Well, I thought about what we talked about last time, about Kate and I not spending time together as a couple talking and not worrying about all the problems and practical things. So I arranged for my mother to mind the kids on Saturday night and I took Kate out for dinner. It was funny because she was expecting me to tell her something bad. She asked, "OK, what is the catch? We never do this," but after we got over her suspicions it was great. We just talked about life and how her new project is going, and she gave me some really good ideas about something at my work. Funny, it was like it used to be, helping each other. Anyway, we decided to go on a date once a month.

THERAPIST: Did going on your date make a difference throughout the rest of the week?

HUSBAND: Yeah, it seemed that we were more relaxed, less likely to bite each other's head off. I'm not really sure why but I was more patient with her and I think she with me.

THERAPIST: Now that you think about it, why do you think you were more patient this week?

HUSBAND: [Pause] I guess that I realized that the marriage was worth saving, that after Saturday night and having some fun again, I guess I realized it was worth it.

Coping with Problems

When people are introduced to solution-focused therapy, they often see it as a form of positive thinking, as being out of touch with the reality of their problems, or being in denial of the many external oppressive forces that burden marginalized groups (such as poverty, racism, etc.). This, however, is an oversimplified view. A good solution-focused therapist is not problem phobic and takes very seriously

---

Practice Exercise 4.2a.
Learning from the Past: Exceptions

Think of an ongoing problem that you have been dealing with over the past few years (personal or professional).

1. Now think of an exception—a time or situation in which the problem was less or didn't happen at all.

    Spend some time exploring what happened during this exception.
    What did you say/do/feel/think differently?
    What did others say/do/feel/think differently?
    What else?

2. What "clues" does this exception reveal about the solution to the problem?

    What does it teach you?
    What would you like to learn from it?
    What skills, strengths, and resources does it reveal about you and others who are supportive to you in this problem?
    What could you do to bring about a similar exception in your life again?

---

the reality that problems do exist in clients' lives. He or she realizes that many clients are battling with oppression, prejudice, and discrimination.

A solution-focused therapist believes that strengths-based solution building rather than deficit-focused problem solving is a more effective and time-sensitive way to help clients. In particular, the shift is from exploring the nature of problems and how they affect or damage clients to exploring how clients have responded and coped with these problems. Such a reorientation of the conversation can be more empowering as it assumes an active coping response on the part of the client rather than a passive reaction to life problems. Consider the following example of a client coping with depression.

THERAPIST: Sounds like things can be pretty bad for you sometimes. I'm sorry to hear that.

CLIENT: Yeah. I can feel pretty low sometimes. Black thoughts can take me over.

THERAPIST: Mmm . . . What keeps you going through these difficult times?

CLIENT: I don't know. . . . I just don't want to let it beat me.

THERAPIST: You don't want to let the depression beat you.

Client: No, I don't . . .

THERAPIST: How do you stop it beating you? How do you keep the black thoughts at bay?

CLIENT: Well . . . when it's pretty bad . . . I try to say to myself . . . "Listen, this will get better. . . . I'll get through this."

THERAPIST: I see. So you remind yourself that the mood will lift and that it will be better soon. What else do you do?

CLIENT: Sometimes I think that my wife will be home soon . . . and that gives me something to look forward to.

THERAPIST: Ah, I see . . . thinking of something nice in the future, something to look forward to, like your wife coming home makes a difference.

A focus on coping highlights the fact that despite having problems, clients still have access to a number of strengths and resources that allow them to survive and manage their lives. These coping strengths, which are often forgotten or not fully accessed, provide clues to creating a solution and/or helping the client live more resourcefully in the face of the problem. In addition, the shift in therapeutic conversation from "impact" to "coping" can be beneficial to clients. Such a strengths-based conversation may be experienced as more liberating and empowering as it gives voice to the story of clients' creative coping in the face of the problems that afflict them.

Focusing on coping gives us a different lens through which to view difficult past events that have occurred in clients' lives. For example, if a client describes her parents as being very cold toward her as a child, rather than simply asking how they were cold to her or how this made her feel or how this affected her, we can ask how she coped with what happened, what this experience taught her, or what decisions she has made about the type of parent she wants to be given her own childhood.

Allan Wade (1997) takes this approach farther when working with clients who have experienced violence and severe trauma. He has found that people resist the violence that has happened to them in

Practice Exercise 4.2b. Learning from the Past: Coping

Think of an ongoing problem that you have been dealing with over the last few years (personal or professional).

1. Now think of a time when the problem occurred severely, when it was at its worst in your life. Spend some time thinking about how you got through this time.

   How did you cope?
   What did you say/do/feel/think that helped you cope?
   What did others say/do/feel/think that helped you cope?
   What else?

2. What resources did you draw upon?

   What did you learn from this time?
   What clues does this experience reveal to you about the best way to cope with this problem?
   How would you like to cope/respond to the problem the next time it occurs?

simple, everyday ways that he calls "small acts of living." For example, a woman who has been raped may cope by freezing her body and putting her thoughts elsewhere, or a child who has been sexually abused by her father may respond by being defiant and troublesome to her parents.

Such responses are often undervalued and unappreciated in subsequent psychotherapy. Indeed, they are often thought of as maladaptive coping responses or symptoms of problems (such as dissociation in the former example and behavioral problems in the latter). Wade (1997), however, argues that these responses are better framed as heroic acts of resistance and explored in therapy through this strengths-based lens. He argues that shifting the therapeutic conversation from asking how clients have been damaged or affected by past trauma to asking how they have responded to or resisted the event can uncover stories of creative coping and resistance on the part of clients, which in themselves can be liberating and therapeutic to express. Wade argues that through this process, people begin to experience themselves as stronger, more insightful, and more capable of responding effectively to the difficulties that brought them to therapy.

A focus on coping inherently implies that people can be strengthened and can learn from negative and traumatic experiences, as well as be damaged by them, but this is not to justify or approve such experiences. Furman and Ahola (1992) use the metaphor of healing bones to illustrate this:

> Even if fractured bones may sometimes become stronger after healing, it does not justify fracturing bones. However strong a bone may become from recovering from an accidental fracture we do all in our power to protect ourselves and others from such injury. (p. 37)

Such an approach is pragmatic: We cannot reverse the adversities we have experienced or the terrible things that have happened to us, all we can do is choose our response to what has happened. We can choose to learn from our adversities, choose to let them make us wiser and more compassionate, and choose to bear witness and give support to others who have experienced similar events.

Pretherapy and Presession Change

A very specific example of looking for past successes or improvement is presession change. Originators of the solution-focused model noted when clients were asked what changes had occurred between the decision to come to therapy and the first session, over 60 percent reported positive changes. Things were already changing for the better prior to beginning therapy (Weiner-Davis, de Shazer, and Gingerich, 1987). SFT believes it is crucial to focus on these small, positive changes as a way of building steps toward a solution. Since these changes occurred outside therapy, the client can take total responsibility for them. The positive changes, if highlighted, may then help clients find solutions to their problems or ways of coping with their situation. If discussed, these changes help clients notice what they are already doing right and encourages them to continue these behaviors.

In support of the importance of presession change, research was conducted with clients who scheduled a first appointment and then did not show or cancelled the appointment. These clients were contacted and asked why they did not attend. More than one-third of these clients reported they did not attend because improvements had already occurred (McKeel, 1996). Other research suggests that cli-

Practice Exercise 4.3. Finding Resources in Your Family

Many problem-focused therapies trace the origins of problems in clients' relationships to their parents and families of origin. It is interesting to reverse this process and to look for inherited strengths from (or learned from) the people who brought you up.

If you suffered abuse as a child, it can be helpful to explore which of the people you encountered in the past provided some protection and support or helped you cope despite the difficulties.

This exercise may aid your own development as a therapist. It can also be adapted as a creative exercise to be done with clients.

1. Make a list of significant people in your life when you were growing up. Identify those who you remember as being supportive to you.

   What positive influence did each of these people have on your life?
   What did you learn from them?
   What did you value about them?

2. Think about some of the positive qualities you have identified about your work as a therapist. (You may wish to revisit the previous exercises.)

   Who else in your family shares these qualities?
   Who helped you develop these qualities?
   Who inspired you to believe/act/think this way?

3. If upon completing this exercise you recall abusive or sad experiences in your childhood, consider the following:

   If you could change what happened to you, what would you change?
   How did you cope with these experiences?
   Who in your family supported you through these times?
   Who outside your family supported you? (People often identify others, such as teachers or coaches, as being helpful or protective of them.)
   If you feel these experiences left you with a negative "script" or legacy, how would you like to change it?
   What have you learned or would you like to learn from this experience?

ents displaying presession change are four times as likely to finish therapy successfully (Beyebach et al., 1996). Therefore, it is important for a therapist to ask questions during the first session about things that may have been helpful in relation to the problem since the client decided to attend therapy. Consider the following dialogue example of presession change being explored.

THERAPIST: Before we begin, I would be interested to know if there has been anything that you have been doing since you decided to come for counseling that you think has helped you with the problem that has brought you here today.

CLIENT: [Pause] Well, I guess since I decided to come to counseling I have begun to tell people . . . you know . . . tell people about what a tough time I've been having lately.

THERAPIST: And that has helped?

CLIENT: Yeah, well I have had some really great responses. Like since I told my mother about the sadness, how very sad I get, well she has been great . . . calling me and talking to me about it and even telling me about herself . . . stuff I didn't even know about.

THERAPIST: Really, so gaining support from people has helped you recently. Is there anyone else who has been helpful in your coping?

CLIENT: My boyfriend and friends have been great. One girlfriend, Sue, she was the one who pushed me to come here, but since I started telling people I haven't felt so alone in it, like such a freak. People have been pretty good, really good in just listening.

THERAPIST: So telling people about your problem and gaining their support has really helped. In what way do you think it has helped?

CLIENT: Well, I know I'm not alone, and that really helps.

The therapist highlights things that the client has been doing since making the appointment that have helped her. The therapist does no more than elicit these strategies and reinforce with the client that they were helpful. The client can then make the choice if she feels that continuing these behaviors would be helpful to her.

Scaling Progress

Scaling questions are a useful way of helping clients see the progress they have already made toward their goals and to focus them creatively on the resources, skills, and strengths they have accessed during this progress. Standard examples of scaling questions include:

- On a scale of 1 to 10, where 10 is when you completely achieve your goal and 1 is the farthest away you have ever been, where would you place yourself now?
- On a scale of 1 to 10, where 1 is the worst things have been and 10 is the best, where would you place yourself today?

There is no right answer to a scaling question. It does not matter whether the client answers 1, 5, or even 9. The therapeutic power of a scaling question is revealed by open-ended, follow-up questions that facilitate clients in describing the progress they have already made, identifying new strengths, skills, and resources, and formulating the next small step toward their goals. For example, if a client answers 4 to one of the previous sample questions the therapist might respond:

- What makes you think you have progressed that far?
- What things have you already done that helped you get to 4?
- What moved you from 3 to 4?

Even if clients rate themselves very low on a scale, for example 1 or 0, there are still a number of solution-focused ways to keep the conversation focused on solution talk. For example, the therapist could follow up with:

- It sounds pretty bad today. How are you coping?
- Have you always been at that point on the scale? Were there times when you were slightly farther on? What was different about those times?
- This is the lowest you have been, yet you still came here today believing that something can be different. What gives you that hope?
- What is the smallest change you need to give you the smallest sign of hope?

Sometimes when a client is feeling low we don't need to force the conversation into solution talk. Sometimes we simply need to hear and acknowledge the client's feelings. We need to be sensitive, to go at the client's pace, and momentarily abandon our techniques and ideas of change, if needed.

Adapting Scaling Questions

Scaling questions are one of the simplest and most versatile of all solution-focused techniques. By representing them pictorially, they can be grasped by children as young as four. For example, using a picture with happy and sad faces connected by a line, a child can be asked to mark how close he or she is to the happy face, or by drawing a mountain with a sunny summit and a pathway weaving upward, a child can be asked how far he or she has already climbed toward the summit.

Significant Others and Scaling

Even if a client is attending the therapy session alone, the therapist can ask scaling questions about significant people in the client's life; the people who are important in the client's journey toward his or her goals. This can provide a new perspective on the therapy and enrich the detail of the desired solution. In addition, clients may have other people attribute strengths to them that they recognize in themselves, but feel shy or uncomfortable about describing. Examples of these questions include:

- If I were to ask your partner, where would he or she say you are on a scale between 1 and 10 in achieving your goal?

If they say that the partner's is higher than theirs, you could ask:

- What makes them more confident?
- Why do they think you have gone farther?

If they say that the partner's score is lower, you could ask:

- What would it take to convince them that you are moving toward your goal?

Both these questions are eliciting once again, strengths, positives—small steps that can help move toward a goal.

Scaling Questions Example

Consider the following case example, where a scaling question is used to start a conversation about the client's progress.

THERAPIST: On a scale between one and ten, where one is the worst that things have been for you and ten is the problem completely resolved, where would you say you are now?

CLIENT: [Pause] At three at the moment, I'd say.

THERAPIST: Really. So things aren't as bad as they once were. What makes you think that you have moved on?

CLIENT: The fact that I'm back to work now is a big step. When I was at one things were falling apart and I was not even going to work. It is a miracle I didn't lose my job.

THERAPIST: What do you think helped you back to work?

CLIENT: One day my little girl said: "Mom, why are you not going to work anymore?" This really threw me because I didn't realize she even noticed anything different. From that moment on I began to think about how my little girl saw me. So at the moment that is my motivation, to make sure that I'm proud of how my little girl sees me. I think this is the biggest factor that has me back to work and functioning again.

THERAPIST: It sounds like that was a pretty important moment for you, deciding that you want to make her proud. How have you been able to do that so far?

CLIENT: I'm now back at work, and taking care of her myself. My mother does not need to stay with us anymore; I'm taking care of Elaine myself.

THERAPIST: Sounds like you have made quite a lot of progress already, taking care of Elaine and getting back to work. Anything else you can think of?

CLIENT: [Pause] I've made a decision not to put myself in danger anymore, not for anyone. When my partner used to hit me I always put up with it, but not anymore. I've told him to stay away, or I'll get a barring order, and I really mean it this time.

THERAPIST: Good, you have really taken a firm stance for the better. What is helping you make these changes and keep to them?

CLIENT: Any time I get weak, I just go look at Elaine. She is enough to keep me on the right track.

Celebrating Change

A critical part of the cycle of goal achievement and change is celebration. The most positive and enjoyable way we can learn from the past and increase our rate of progress is not by criticizing or focusing on setbacks, but by noting and celebrating achievements and positive change, including small gains and steps in the right direction. It is very useful to reflect upon and view the past through this celebratory rather than critical lens. Such a reviewing can help us realize how far we have actually come. Too often people move quickly onto the next goal, dream, or ambition without giving themselves time to celebrate the goals, dreams, and ambitions that have already been fulfilled

---

Practice Exercise 4.4. How Far Have You Come?

Take time to reflect on your therapeutic practice. Think back to when you first started thinking about becoming a therapist. What were your hopes and dreams at that time? On a scale of 1 to 10, where 1 is when you first started thinking about being a therapist and 10 is actively doing the job you want to be doing, where are you now?

1	2	3	4	5	6	7	8	9	10

What has helped you to come as far as you have?
What are the steps you have taken to achieve this progression through the scale?
How have you marked or celebrated the progress you have made?
If you have not celebrated this progress, how would you like to celebrate now?
Who has helped you progress?
Who are your supporters?
How have you acknowledged their support/credited them with contributing to your achievements?
If you have not had a chance to do this, how could you do it now?

through hard work and courage. Giving past triumphs consideration may help us realize what we did to encourage these events to happen in the first place. This may motivate our quest for future dreams.

Essentially, the dynamic of solution-focused therapy is one of noticing and celebrating positive change. Insoo Kim Berg (1994) describes how this change can be identified and reinforced using the EARS technique. The therapist should first elicit examples of progress, then amplify and reinforce them, and finally start again with a new example of progress.

Case Study 4.1

Consider the following client who has been referred to the outpatient clinic of the psychiatric ward of a hospital after a suicide attempt. The referral notes mention that she attempted suicide one week ago. She was admitted to the hospital and spent the past week there before the psychiatrist felt she was safe enough to discharge. She has been referred to the day hospital for counseling and support to overcome her difficulties.

Take time to reflect on this case, and consider how you would work with the young woman in a way that respects how far she has already come. Write down your ideas and suggestions and then compare them with the key at the end of the book. Remember, the important thing is to generate ideas that may be helpful to the client.

Sue is a twenty-five-year-old single woman who describes herself as coping and managing for the most part. She works for a bank and is very proud of her achievements at work. She is confused about what has led to such a difficult past few months that resulted in her making a suicide attempt. She would not have considered herself a depressed person in the past, but has recently felt overwhelmed with loneliness and a sense of "things not being worth it." After several months of feeling as if she was "spinning downward with no one noticing," she made the suicide attempt. Sue lives with her mother and two brothers. Her father died several years ago. She describes her family as supportive, yet her main source of support is her friends. Sue has been honest and open with her friends and family regarding her hospitalization and current need for support, and states that people have gone beyond being helpful in their support. She says that she would like to get on with her life, but not to have these feelings of loneliness in the future. She feels as if she needs meaning in her life.

EARS Technique

1. **E**licit: What has been better?
                 What's different?
2. **A**mplify: Who else noticed this change?
                 How did you get the idea to do this?
3. **R**einforce: Wow, that's quite an achievement.
                 How were you able to do it?
4. **S**tart over: What else is better?
                 What else is different?

Consider the following example to illustrate this process:

THERAPIST: That sounds like it was a big step for you, congratulations for being brave enough to go! How did it come about?

CLIENT: I just started thinking that I can't do this alone, I mean staying off the drink. It is just too hard and all my friends are drinkers, so it is not like they are going to sit home with me on Friday night. So I thought I better find something else to do. That is how it started, just wanting to have another place to go besides the bar.

THERAPIST: [Leaning in and curious] Yeah, but what a big step to take to go to AA. How did you get the courage to go the first night?

CLIENT: I almost didn't. I walked up and down the street several times before I went in. The thing that finally did it was I passed this homeless guy on the street; he was drinking and I thought if I don't get my act together, I'm going to be him. I really scared myself into it.

THERAPIST: So you were able to get yourself there even though it was pretty hard.

CLIENT: Only the first night was hard; now it is easy. I've been going every day since I saw you last and it really makes all the difference.

THERAPIST: You really sound like you have come a long way since we last met—a really long way. . . . Congratulations!

CLIENT: I feel it too. I know I have a long way to go but I know I'm at least heading there now.

Summary

In this chapter we have looked at the clues the solution leaves in the present and the past, particularly in the form of exceptional times when the problem did not exist, or implicitly in the heroic, though often unnoticed, coping strategies of the client in response to the excesses of the problem. We have emphasized how important it is to value and appreciate the distance the client has already traveled on the journey to a solution, no matter how apparently small this distance seems. In the next chapter we consider the next stage in moving to a solution and ask the question: "What is the next step?"

Chapter 5

What Is the Next Step?

Even a journey of a thousand miles starts with a single step.

Chinese proverb

To a great mind, nothing is little.

Sherlock Holmes

We have already discussed many of the clues solution detectives look for as they collaborate with their clients to solve a problem and to unmask the solution. These clues include the importance of connecting with clients, identifying strengths, discovering goals, and appreciating the progress clients have made. We now look at putting all these clues together to identify, with clients, the next step. We consolidate all the information that we have gleaned into a small, achievable step that clients are prepared, willing, and able to take toward their goals.

Scaling the Next Step

As stated previously, scaling questions are probably among the most versatile and universally helpful techniques in solution-focused therapy. In Chapter 4 we saw how they can be used to elicit the steps a client has already taken toward his or her goal. We now consider how they can be used to identify the next small steps of change. As described in Chapter 4, a typical use of the question would be as follows:

- On a scale of 1 to 10, where 1 is the worst things have been and 10 the best, where would you place yourself at the moment?

To identify small achievable steps the following questions can be used:

- How would you know you had moved one point (or even half a point) on the scale?
- What would be the first sign that you were moving forward?

If the client is concerned that he or she is going to slip the next week, the question can become:

- What can you do next week to keep yourself at the same point?
- What needs to happen so you are confident of keeping the progress you have already made?

Scaling questions can also involve significant people in a client's life:

- Who else would notice that you had moved one point forward on the scale? What would they notice?

Now consider Practice Exercise 5.1 as an example of identifying the next step in your developing practice as a therapist.

Practice Exercise 5.1. Identifying the Next Step

This exercise is a follow-up from Practice Exercise 4.4 in which you explored, using scaling, the progress you had achieved toward your goal of being a therapist. The aim now is to project yourself into the future to identify the "next small step" toward your goal.

1. What needs to happen now to help you progress one point on the scale toward your goal?
2. What would be the first small step toward your goal?
3. What would be the first sign that would tell you that you were beginning to move toward your goal?
4. What could you do next week (or even today) that would ensure you are making progress?

Attending to Motivation

Often clients find it hard to identify the next step toward their goals or, if they do, they feel such a step is beyond their reach and feel hopeless about making even the smallest move forward. From a solution-focused perspective, these problems can be understood in terms of a client's motivation toward the agreed therapeutic goal. In solution-focused therapy, motivation is not conceived as something fixed or intrinsic to the client, but rather as a shared creation between therapist and client. The level of motivation says more about the context of the therapy and how successful the therapeutic relationship is at a particular point in time. Clients will be motivated if they feel the therapy is centered on their goals, uses their strengths and skills to make progress, and if they feel the therapist has their best interests at heart. The onus is on the therapist to ensure that he or she is doing what they can to create this motivational context.

The solution-focused model describes three levels of motivation that categorize the therapist-client relationship at any given time, notably customer, complainant, and visitor (Berg and Miller, 1992; de Shazer, 1988).

Customer

At the customer level of motivation, therapy flows easily. Client and therapist have identified a clear problem and goal toward which they are collaboratively working. Clients crucially believe that they can be effective in solving their problems; by changing their own thoughts and actions they can bring about desired change. They are cooperative and active in therapy and easily identify the next steps on the road to change. Using a shopping metaphor, Miller (1998) describes clients at this level of motivation as being "ideal customers" who come into the "therapy shop" with a relatively clear idea of what they want to buy and an expectation that they will be able to get it in your shop.

Complainant

At the complainant level of motivation, therapy can sometimes feel stuck. A complainant is someone who thinks there is a problem, is motivated to change it, but sees it as something beyond his or her control and as something to do with how other people are behaving and thinking. The therapeutic relationship can often be in conflict as clients want the therapist to "do something" on their behalf or to persuade someone else to change. Miller (1998) describes complainants as being like "browsers" in a shop. They have a need to buy something, but only a vague idea of what they exactly want, and they aren't clear if they will be able to get it in your shop.

Visitor

At the visitor level of motivation, therapy can be difficult to get started. Clients either do not feel that the identified problems are an issue for them or they are uninterested in the identified goal of the therapy. Thus, they are not really motivated to identify the next small step or, indeed, to take action. If they do get to the counselor or therapist's office, it is generally because they are sent or coerced by a third party. Using the shopping metaphor, visitors can be likened to "window shoppers" (Miller, 1998). They have not yet ventured inside the shop and only have a vague idea that they actually want to buy anything. An example of a complainant is a mother who is very concerned about her son's drug abuse and insists he attend counseling. The son in this case, who does not believe he has a drug abuse problem, can be described as a visitor.

Visitor, complainant, and customer levels of motivation can be thought of as being developmentally related to one another. Often clients pass through each stage as they solve problems in their lives. They may first be visitors, having no particular awareness of a problem or of wanting something different. When such awareness is awakened they may not feel influential in creating change, blame others for their predicament, and thus become complainants. Finally, they may discover their own effectiveness with regard to certain goals and thus become customers.

In the example of the drug-abusing son: from visitor, he may advance to complainant due to his mother's pressure and restriction of his independence, and blame her excessive nagging and controlling behavior. However, he may finally discover his own effectiveness by communicating with his mother, understanding her concerns, and convincing her of his need for independence. He is now a customer.

Visitor, complainant, and customer levels of motivation have links to the stages of change model developed by Prochaska, DiClemente, and associates (Prochaska and DiClemente, 1992; Prochaska, DiClemente, and Norcross, 1992) who proposed six stages of change as outlined in Table 5.1. Visitor and complainant levels of motivation correspond approximately to precontemplation and contemplation respectively, while the four latter stages of change relate to different types of customer interactions (see Table 5.1).

When clients are at complainant or visitor levels of motivation, they are likely to find it hard to identify the next step that they are willing to take toward their goals. They are simply not ready for an action plan and/or not clear about what they can do differently to bring about the desired changes, and thus are unlike customers.

When working with complainants or visitors, the next step centers on simply improving their motivation. The aim is to identify a step that may help them move toward being a customer. This usually does not involve doing anything different, but rather simply consider other views of their situations or appreciate other perspectives. However, a step toward thinking differently can represent a big shift when you consider their starting place.

To facilitate this, scaling questions can often be used creatively. In the next chapter we will explore in more detail the broader issues of engaging complainants and visitors. Consider now Practice Exercise 5.2 for experiential examples on how to improve your motivation.

TABLE 5.1. Motivation Levels

Solution-Focused Therapy	Stages of Change
Visitor	Precontemplation
Complainant	Contemplation
Customer	Preparation
	Action
	Maintenance
	Termination

Source: Prochaska and DiClemente, 1992.

Practice Exercise 5.2. Improving Your Motivation

Visitor to Complainant

1. Think of a possible change/goal in your personal life at which you would be at visitor level motivation: something that may be beneficial to change but doesn't worry you greatly and to which you have not given much thought. This could be something that significant others think is important for you to do, such as giving up smoking, reducing drinking, increasing leisure time, eating a more healthy diet, exercising more, or something completely different.
2. Imagine you are sent to therapy by a court order to work on this goal. This will help you empathize with the many clients who are sent to therapy! What therapist qualities would be most helpful to you?
3. On a scale of 1 to 10, how motivated are you to work on this goal (where 1 is no motivation [e.g., a visitor] and 10 is highly motivated)? If you answer higher than 1, what causes you to be this motivated? Why are you at 2 rather than 1?
4. What would cause you to move one point on the scale? What would make you become a little more concerned about this goal or want it that little bit more, e.g., what would help you become a complainant?

Complainant to Customer

5. Think of a different problem that concerns or worries you greatly, one which you feel you have no personal control over, or for which other people must change first in order for resolution to occur. This could include personal issues, such as a difficult boss or family member, or issues in your community such as homelessness or crime or indeed any personal issues that are easy to complain about and feel difficult to change.
6. Imagine talking to a therapist who is going to help you solve this problem. What approach from the therapist would be helpful?
7. On a scale of 1 to 10, how confident are you of your ability to make progress toward this goal, where 1 is no confidence and 10 is highly confident? If you answer higher than 1, what causes you to be this confident? Why are you at 2 rather than 1, for example?
8. What would cause you to move one point on the scale? What would make you become a little more confident about your own ability to make progress? (e.g., what would help you advance to customer?)

(continued)

(continued)

Tip: Instead of focusing on the problem, begin focusing on your response to it. Think of what influence you have. How can you think differently about this problem and your response to it that might allow you to act differently? For example, instead of getting upset when your boss undermines you, you could decide not to let it bother you and reply assertively; or rather than just ignoring homelessness, you could take action by writing to your local representatives or contribute time or money to a local charity.

Confidence Scaling

When clients feel distant from their goals or appear powerless about making progress, as complainants often are, it can be useful to ask a scaling question about their confidence to move on. This question may elicit new resources and strengths (e.g., beliefs and optimism) which can help things move on, for example:

- How confident are you between 1 and 10 that you are able to move on to the next step toward your goal?

Depending on the answer you have the choice of the normal follow-up questions:

- What makes you that confident? (Why are you at 2 rather than 1?)
- What will make you that little bit more confident?
- What will move you one point on?

Confidence scaling questions can also involve important people in the client's life:

- If I were to ask your partner, how confident would he or she be on the same scale about you reaching that goal?

If the partner is rated higher on the scale it could be asked:

- What makes him or her more confident?
- What does the partner see in you that gives him or her that confidence?
- How could the partner convince you to be more confident?

If the partner is rated lower, the following might be asked:

- What makes you more confident?
- What do you know about yourself that makes you more confident?
- What would make him or her more confident?

Motivation Scaling

Even when clients feel far away from their goals and lack confidence in getting there, scaling questions can be used to uncover their desire for change. Consider the following possibilities:

- On a scale between 1 and 10, how much do you want to get along better with your partner?
- On a scale between 1 and 10, how much do you want your son to stop taking drugs?

Even complainants who are very pessimistic about change often score themselves high on these scales. By using follow-up questions such as "what makes you want this goal so much?" we can put clients in touch with the strength of their convictions and reveal the positive motivations that underlie the current problems (for example, the clients' love and concern for their families). This can help garner resources for change. Motivation scaling can also help identify clients at the visitor level of motivation and give you an opportunity to renegotiate the therapeutic goal.

- On a scale between 1 and 10 how much do you want to give up drugs?
- On a scale between 1 and 10 how willing are you to work on solving this problem?
- Who most wants you to give up drinking?
- Where would you put his or her motivation on the same scale?
- What makes him or her more motivated? (Or less motivated?)

If clients score low on the first two questions, it is a good indication that they are visitors. This allows the therapist to renegotiate more client-centered goals which clients are willing to work on. For example, the teenager sent to therapy by his mother to stop his drug abuse may not be motivated to stop using drugs but very motivated to get his parents off his back and regain his independence. Scaling techniques are very powerful in helping clients to identify small steps, changes, and signs that indicate that they are making progress or that the therapy is moving to a more meaningful client-centered goal which the clients are motivated to work toward.

A Structure for a Solution-Focused Session

A simple structure for a solution-focused session, which mirrors the titles of Chapters 2 through 5, is as follows:

1. Build a therapeutic alliance (Starting where the client is at)
2. Establish a goal (Where does the client want to go?)
3. Appreciate progress (How far has he or she already come?)
4. Make progress (What is the next step?)
   a. Take a therapeutic break
   b. Let client evaluate the session
   c. Therapist gives feedback
   d. Plan/set a task

This chapter is essentially concerned with Stage 4—negotiating with clients a realistic next step toward their goals. As you can see from the just stated structure, this process can be aided by taking a break during the session time.

Practice Exercise 5.3. A Letter of Commitment

The purpose of this exercise is to increase your commitment to the goals you want to achieve and to encourage you to take steps to achieve these goals.

1. Think of a goal you are working on at present. Once again, you can choose the goal of developing your practice as a therapist or another personal goal.
2. Write a letter to yourself describing clearly how you want the future to develop and what steps you see as necessary to move toward your goal. The important part of this letter is to explain to the reader (yourself) your commitment to the goal.

   • Why do you want to progress this way in your life?
   • How will it impact you if you do continue to head toward the things you want?
   • How will achieving these things benefit you as a person?

Be clear and detailed in your letter about how you will achieve these life goals and what positive benefits you will derive from them. Try to convince the reader (yourself) of your strong commitment and dedication to these goals.

3. Once you have finished the letter, keep a copy of it in a safe place so you can refer to it occasionally to remind yourself of your commitment to these changes/developments in your life.

Taking a Therapeutic Break

If therapy is to be successful, the process has to have some impact on the client's life. A successful session involves a client thinking, feeling, or doing something differently, whether a major life change such as deciding to change careers or a small shift in thinking such as remembering a happy memory from childhood. Because this perceived difference is so important, it can be very powerful to identify and reflect upon it before the client leaves the therapy room.

Taking a therapeutic break can be very helpful in this regard by distinguishing between the action of the session and an evaluation.

Such a pause can draw attention to the importance of the next step and what the client is doing/thinking/feeling differently.

The concept of a therapeutic break originally came from the family therapy tradition, where therapists often work in teams (Minuchin, 1974; Minuchin et al., 1967), and has been a key feature in the development of the original solution-focused model. Among other things, it has been deemed useful to give the therapist time to reflect about the session, to consult with colleagues, and to devise helpful therapeutic tasks.

Toward a Client-Directed Break

Extensive research on treatment compliance indicates that ideas and plans generated by clients are those most likely to be carried out and to effect change (Hubble, Duncan, and Miller, 1999; Duncan and Miller, 2000). For this reason, it is important not only for therapists to reflect and plan during the therapeutic break, but for clients to be encouraged to do likewise. Taking a break gives a client time to reflect and think about the session. It also punctuates the session, allowing the client specific time to plan or reflect on its key moments. Indeed, in response to the growing interest in creating collaborative interventions, in our work we have introduced the use of a more "client-directed" session break (Sharry et al., 2001). Clients are encouraged to use the break to reflect on what has happened, to generate their own conclusions, and even to assign themselves homework if they wish. To facilitate this, how the break is introduced to the client is important. We suggest the following:

THERAPIST: Near the end of the session we take a five-minute break. This is to give you time to think and reflect about what we have discussed and to pick out the important ideas that came up or to make any decisions or plans. You might also like to think about whether this session has been useful and how you would like us to be further involved. While you're thinking, I will consult with my team for their thoughts and also think about what we have discussed. If you would like to hear some of my ideas, please ask me when I come back.

The emphasis is on the client thinking, reflecting, and possibly planning. (There is no emphasis on this if the client is not at that stage of motivation.) In addition, there is no assumption that therapy need continue. This reflects a core assumption of brief therapy—that each session could be the last or that a small number of sessions may be enough for a client. While this may not be the case for all clients, within the solution-focused brief therapy approach the decision about the length of therapy is decided by the client rather than prescribed by the therapist.

A session break introduced in this manner recognizes the central role of the client as the agent of therapeutic change and the most important solution detective. It also allows clients' ideas and plans to be evaluated prior to those of the therapist and helps them to identify their own strengths and resources. In this way clients direct the help they receive rather than simply being told what they need. Finally, a client-directed break is collaborative: clients are active in the therapeutic intervention and the burden on the therapist to have the right answer is reduced. The responsibility for successful therapy is shared between therapist and client. Session breaks need not involve the therapist leaving the room. They also can be used as punctuation points in the session, where the therapist invites the client to pause and take stock of what has been discussed.

Such breaks can be introduced as follows:

THERAPIST: Let's take a moment to think about what we have discussed today. I'm interested to know what stood out for you today, what you thought was important, and what ideas you want to take away. If it's OK with you I'll make notes as you speak to record what you say.

Whether the therapist leaves the room or stays and reflects with the client, the essential point in a collaborative or client-directed session break is that the therapist first seeks the views and thoughts of the client in evaluating the session and constructing a plan of action.

Client Evaluation of Session

After a session break, clients' thoughts and ideas are considered most important, and are discussed first, prior to those of the therapist. This can be done by simply asking: "What ideas or thoughts have you had during the break?" At this review point it can be useful to make case notes. Recording client ideas in a written form gives them special validation and status. Equally, the act of writing slows down the process, reinforcing the key insights generated by giving them extra time and attention.

Therapist Feedback

After clients' ideas have been explored, there is an opportunity for the therapist to give constructive feedback in the form of compliments; the therapist highlights one or two strengths he or she has noticed about the client and feeds them back. The process of giving positive feedback can be most powerful when a quality initially thought of as a deficit is presented as a strength, possibly containing the seeds of the solution. For example, we often pathologize mothers as having overprotective or enmeshed relationships with their children. This can be reframed as demonstrating a desire for a very close relationship with their children, or indicating efforts to protect them. Equally, a father who is seen as overly critical of his children can be reframed as reflecting a desire for them to achieve their potential, or as his ability to know their capabilities.

The therapist should also be optimistic and upbeat in his or her feedback, predicting and picking out examples of change. The aim is a sort of cheerleading or coaching effect, helping the client adopt an optimistic view in his or her own life. Outcome research indicates that the ability to be optimistic or hopeful about change, on the part of the therapist and client, is a key indicator of successful therapy (Hubble, Duncan, and Miller, 1999; Duncan and Miller, 2000). When presenting feedback and predicting change, it is essential to be genuine. It must be presented congruently and reflected in your body language and tone of voice. If you are unsure about a certain example of positive feedback, then don't give it. Instead find other examples of positive feedback you can genuinely give your clients.

Setting a Task

After constructive feedback is delivered, the therapist can collaboratively create with the client an action plan which can be carried out between visits. Although such a plan is only likely to be success-

Practice Exercise 5.4.
Gaining Support/Celebrating Change

It is important to have as much support as possible when we are working toward our goals. The people around us can contribute to our successes and help us celebrate when we reach our goals. Take time to reflect on the people in your life who will support you in your quest to become a solution-focused therapist. These may include family members, work colleagues, classmates, and even clients. The list will be specific to you.

1.
2.
3.
4.
5.

Think about how you might celebrate with these supportive individuals when you have progressed toward your goals. In what ways could you thank them for supporting you in your quest to become a solution-focused therapist?

1.
2.
3.
4.
5.

Source: Adapted from Furman and Ahola (1997).

ful if it builds on the ideas and thoughts of the client (Hubble, Duncan, and Miller, 1999; Duncan and Miller, 2000), this is not to discount the input of the therapist. In some cases, clients are able to generate their own plan forward, but more generally they seek some ideas from the therapist. The resultant plan is best conceived as a "cocreation," drawing on the best ideas from therapist and client. If the therapist does make a suggestion, it is important that this is matched to the client's level of motivation at that time. While customers may welcome a task that involves them doing something different, complainants and visitors most likely will not.

Complainant Level of Motivation

The complainant is generally burdened by the problem, but sees it as beyond his or her control. He or she is not yet ready to do anything different. The focus at this stage of motivation is on noticing, reflecting, and observing, much like a browser in a shop. You are asking a browser to do what they do best, to take time to examine things closely and to pick out what they like and dislike. A possible observing task might be as follows.

THERAPIST: Between now and the next session, I want you to notice the times the problem gets a little bit better, for example, times you get along better with your son, and just notice what happens, how it comes about, what it is like, etc.

Alternatively, it can be useful to appreciate the impact of the problem on the complainant and to suggest a nurturing task.

THERAPIST: You are dealing with a very difficult problem . . . it is very important that you look after yourself next week so you can be strong enough to combat it. What can you do next week to look after yourself?

Visitor Level of Motivation

Visitors are generally not yet motivated to carry out any tasks. It is suggested that the therapist should simply compliment them for coming and point out any other strengths they have noticed in the visitor's position. The client's level of motivation is dependent on situational and relational factors and it is not always possible to identify clearly. There are a number of tasks, however, that can be applied readily in most situations, with customers, complainants, and sometimes visitors. The most well known of these is the "formula first task" (de Shazer, 1985, 1988).

THERAPIST: Between now and the next session I want you to notice anything good that happens in your life that you would like to continue or have happen again. Maybe you can bring these examples to the next session and we can discuss them.

Case Study 5.1

Read the following description of the Miller family's first counseling session. Imagine that after reading the summary of the session you are taking your therapeutic break. Consider what things you might feed back to the Millers regarding the session. Would you request that they do any homework assignments between sessions? If so, what would you request that they do? How can you give the family credit for the difficult time they have had and give them encouragement for the future?

The Miller family has come to counseling due to continuous disagreements and arguments that have increased in the past few months. It has gotten to the point that Mr. Miller is considering moving out of the family home. The family members are Mr. and Mrs. Miller, their sixteen-year-old son Tim, and twelve-year-old daughter Ann.

During the first session, each member of the family talks about his or her frustration with the decline of his or her relationships. Mr. Miller feels he would rather live away from the family than face a constant battle with his son. Mr. Miller feels his son is "out of control," and does not listen to his parents. He is afraid that Tim will wind up in jail and worse. Mr. Miller often expresses that he is disciplining his son for "his own good" and that "it is out of love." He expresses frustration with his wife because

(continued)

(continued)

she does not support him when he tries to discipline Tim. Mr. Miller feels that the family has turned against him, and he sees no way back.

Mrs. Miller and the children express their concerns for the changes in the house. Mrs. Miller takes a more relaxed approach to parenting and finds her husband's "constant regimented discipline" hard to accept. She feels they should accept that the children, particularly Tim, are growing up and need to make their own decisions. She states that she would be "heartbroken" if her husband moved out, but she does not see any other way for the heated disputes to end. During the session, she tearfully admits she would rather see him leave than for the situation to continue as it is.

Tim and Ann both talk about their wish for things to be more relaxed around the house. They both say they love their father, but find it difficult to "put up with" his constant threats and demands.

What could you feedback to the family after the break?

Develop your own ideas before referring to the key at the back of the book.

Summary

This chapter focused on establishing what the next step is as a client moves toward a therapeutic goal. We have noted that often this is a small step involving a small shift in the client's motivation. This may be as a result of negotiating a more client-centered goal with a client at visitor level of motivation, or inviting a shift in thinking with someone at the complainant level. Generally speaking, all a therapy session has to achieve to be successful is a small step in the right direction. Small movements can create great change. In the next chapter, we consider the times the therapeutic process doesn't appear to be making progress, or worse still, appears to be stuck altogether.

Chapter 6

When Therapy Doesn't Go Well

There is nothing more stimulating than a case where everything goes against you.

Sherlock Holmes

The solution-focused path doesn't always run smoothly. Great solutions are not often found overnight and can involve long journeys with many twists and turns. Even great solution detectives have setbacks and obstacles to overcome. Sometimes we travel down false paths that lead nowhere, sometimes we find ourselves looking for strengths and possibilities as if we were in a desert looking for an oasis. But what distinguishes the great therapists from the others is how they confront obstacles and difficulties. They don't become disillusioned by them, they don't become discouraged, and they don't give into the temptation to become negative and blaming. The great solution-detective persists relentlessly and patiently, seeking with the client the solution that lies in their midst. Great solution detectives are above all flexible—continually adapting themselves to the territory through which they travel.

Drawing on the work of Duncan, Hubble, and Miller (1997), we consider three obstacles which can derail the solution-focused journey, notably when (1) we fail to understand the client's motivation, (2) we "do more of the same" in the face of failure; and (3) we let our own theory get in the way of that of the clients. We also describe a generic supervision Practice Exercise 6.1, which can be useful when faced with a difficult case or when things don't run smoothly. It is also an exercise to help you "stay a customer" as a therapist.

Attending to the Client's Motivation

As discussed in Chapter 5, the solution-focused model describes three levels of motivation that categorize the therapist-client relationship at any given time: customer, complainant, and visitor (Berg and Miller, 1992; de Shazer, 1988). One of the major reasons that the therapeutic alliance falters or is difficult to establish in the first place is that the therapist has not sufficiently understood the client's level of motivation with respect to the therapeutic process. The therapist may relate to clients who are at the visitor or complainant level of motivation as if they were customers, and this can cause the therapy to appear stuck.

Remember, when you work with more than one client, as is the case in family or couple work, individual members are often at very different levels of motivation regarding the same problem. This often leads to conflict and these clients can be experienced as warring with one another. It is important that the therapist does not contribute to this conflict by taking sides, becoming a judge, or valuing one position over another. Rather, it is important to become multipartial: find a way of accommodating and understanding different perspectives and positions. The therapist needs to find a way of establishing an alliance with each family member that accommodates his or her level of motivation and perspective. To illustrate the visitor, complainant, and customer categories, consider Case Example 6.1 involving a family coming to therapy. Try to determine the level of motivation for each of the family members.

Becoming Customers

Customers, complainants, and visitors are not fixed categories, but rather are constructed within a specific therapeutic context. At any given time they indicate how satisfactory the therapeutic contract or goal is and how and if the therapeutic alliance is collaborative. Thus the categories can change rapidly as the context is changed. The aim of the therapist is to try to create the conditions that allow the client to move into the customer level of motivation. Complainants and visitors require different approaches if this is to happen.

Case Example 6.1

Joe is a six-year-old boy brought to therapy by his parents. His mother is worried about him being hyperactive and very demanding, and in particular, the "aggressive streak" she sees in him when he is playing with other children. She is stressed, finds Joe very difficult to manage, and wants him assessed to find out what is wrong. Joe's father thinks she is overreacting and that these are the normal difficulties of managing an active and bright six-year-old boy. This leads to much conflict between the parents, with the mother accusing the father of being uninvolved and undermining, and the father accusing the mother of overreacting and not being able to manage her son. Joe seems confused by the business of coming to therapy and "tunes out" during the family assessment meeting, playing with toys in the corner.

1. The mother is at the complainant level of motivation regarding coming to therapy. She recognizes a problem, notably Joe's hyperactivity and aggression. These problems are framed as belonging to Joe and the implicit suggestion is that she feels Joe needs to change or be treated, and she feels helpless in bringing about the necessary change.
2. The father is at the visitor level of motivation, although perhaps on the borderline of becoming a complainant. He acknowledges that there are some problems, but sees these as being a normal part of childhood, certainly not warranting any particular change or therapy.
3. Like most young children who come to therapy, Joe is at the visitor level of motivation. He is perhaps the least involved and least consulted about the problem and the usual suggested means of solving it—coming to talk about it with a stranger. Young children are often inadvertently sidelined in family therapy. The therapist, more familiar with adult relating, may direct most of the conversation to the parents and it can go over the child's head. Yet Joe's ideas and perspective are equally valid and his involvement in the therapeutic process is as critical as that of the parents in creating a successful outcome.

Engaging Visitors

Rather than confronting a visitor about not being motivated toward a certain goal, the solution-focused therapist works hard to validate and understand the visitor's underlying positive intentions. The aim is to uncover a goal he or she is willing to work on, to discover what he or she wants to do rather than clarify what he or she does not want to do. In Case Example 6.1, the father's perspective can be validated: he does not want his son to be labeled negatively and wants to sort out the family problems independent of therapy. His perspective does not need to be validated in opposition to that of the mother, but rather as different and equally valuable—she wants to find ways of understanding and managing her son's behavior and he wants to do it in a way that does not negatively describe his son and which fosters family independence. Both are valid parenting goals.

Second, although visitors can often be viewed as not cooperating with the therapeutic process, this does not take into account the small steps of cooperation they have already made. For example, in Case Example 6.1, the father, despite his reservations, has come along to the first session. If he hadn't attended the meeting, it could be acknowledged as a positive step that he had not blocked his son's attendance. His motivation can be explored constructively; perhaps he is there to support his partner in managing their son, or because he has an open mind to try something new.

Clients at the visitor level of motivation need to be convinced of the value of the therapeutic process—they need to be shown that it will benefit them. The therapist's role is often one of a good salesperson. As stated in Chapter 5, clients at the visitor level of motivation can be likened to people "window shopping" (Miller, 1998). They have not yet decided to buy anything, but are merely viewing what is offered. Similar to an effective salesperson, the best way for a therapist to respond to people at this level of motivation is to make sure that the products appear attractive and appealing and that they are well advertised to show potential customers the benefits. If they tentatively enter the shop, a good salesperson does not immediately assume they want to buy something. The salesperson takes time to show what is offered in the shop, ensuring that visitors have all the information they need. A good salesperson listens carefully to what visitors want and goes out of the way to custom-make what they need. With a "window shopper," a good salesperson knows it might take several visits before the client "buys" anything. What is important is that clients are welcomed and given sufficient information so that they are intrigued enough to come back.

In addition, the therapist's role for visitors can be likened to that of a good host at a party you have organized, for an important guest whom you don't know well. The guest must be invited and welcomed into the process and, as a good host, you go out of your way to make this important person feel valued and entertained. You make sure to involve the guest in the conversation and to consult his or her views on what is being discussed, all the while being as complimentary and respectful as possible. You explain everything that is new and introduce the guest to people he or she doesn't know. All this is done in a personable, courteous manner.

Children are a special group of clients who are generally at the visitor level of motivation. As with Joe in Case Example 6.1, other people have decided for them and children often feel "tuned out" of the therapeutic process. We need to be especially accommodating as therapists to engage them. We take the role of party host at a children's rather than an adult party.

Simple things such as showing them around the therapy room and having a selection of toys can make a difference. When interviewing a family with a one-way screen or video, it can really help to take time to show the children how the technology works, as this can help put them at ease (and also be great fun!). The therapeutic process needs to be sold to children in a way they can understand—"when you participate we have time to play with whatever toys you want and we have time to talk about worries and anything you want to make better in your family." In addition, many children fear they will be rebuked in therapy. Talking in problem-free interaction, in play or in conversation, finding out what children are good at or enjoy doing, can help create different expectations and alliances from which customer contracts can be established.

The more often the therapist uses the children's language and the more the therapist slows to proceed at their pace, the more children become involved. Directing a family therapy session at the child's level often benefits the parents as well as the child. It helps parents appreciate their child's perspective (often the most valuable aspect of therapy), and simple childlike language can ensure that everyone is on board. Being childlike as a therapist can benefit all the family members (at least that is our excuse!).

Engaging Complainants

People at the complainant level of motivation can feel burdened and powerless in the face of a problem. They need to be supported, nurtured, and understood by the therapist before they can become customers. They are not ready yet, as customers are, to consider how their own actions "cause" the problem (or the solution), and, unlike customers, will experience any "do something differently" task as an extra burden. The first stage for the therapist is to constructively understand where the client is and to make a connection (see Chapter 2). In Case Example 6.1, when engaging the mother (who is at the complainant level of motivation) it is important to take a nonblaming, empathic response toward her position. You can empathize with her difficulties in managing a small child and her worry about whether something is wrong. You can compliment her on her concern for her son, which has led her to take action by coming to therapy.

Clients at the complainant level of motivation are likely to feel helpless and ineffective in the face of the problem. They often frame their goals negatively ("I don't want to be depressed") or in terms of other people's actions ("If only my son would calm down"). They feel powerless to make progress toward them.

Transforming complainants into customers often involves a painstaking reexamination of the data. The aim is not to ask clients to do anything differently but to think differently. The search is for exceptions and coping skills not previously noticed or thought important, but which reveal clients' effectiveness in the face of their problems. Therapy is like a journey through the desert looking for an oasis, or a long search for "buried treasure" (George, 1998), which the therapist inspires the client to believe awaits discovery. Once these gems have

been found and the client has taken credit for them, workable, positive customer goals are easier to establish.

As stated in Chapter 5, complainants are akin to "browsers" in a shop. They are motivated to buy something but don't know exactly what it is. A good salesperson listens carefully and gives them plenty of time. He or she invites them to view all that is offered in the shop and encourages them to notice "other items" (e.g., exceptions, possible goals) in the shop that could be of great value to them.

In Case Example 6.1, to elevate the mother's level of motivation, it is important to take her initial goal of wanting her son assessed seriously. You agree that it is a very good idea to try to attain a helpful understanding of the situation, but explain that you need her help. As you explore the situation, look for exceptions—times where she was able to manage and cope with Joe's behavior. For example, she might find that if she sits with Joe and guides him in play with other children, he is less aggressive. You may also coconstruct with her helpful ideas about what was happening during these times, e.g., understanding that Joe was not simply "aggressive" but rather particularly shy and awkward in dealing with other children. Make sure that she is

---

Case Study 6.1. What's Their Motivation?

Consider the following case examples. Decide the level of motivation for each of these clients and plan how you might establish a customer contract with each of them.

Example A

A mother suddenly finds out that her teenage son is smoking marijuana. An unhelpful argument ensues and consequently the mother insists they both go to therapy. The son reluctantly attends, thinking his mother is overreacting.

Example B

A husband and wife are attending couples' therapy. The wife complains that her husband is working too hard and that he never shows her any affection. The husband says he doesn't come home on account of his wife's nagging. He can't bear how critical she is of him.

credited with these exceptions, for example, her skill in guiding Joe in play and her sensitive understanding of him.

Doing More of the Same

> Madness is doing the same thing over and over again but expecting a different result each time.

Anonymous

One of the forerunners to solution-focused therapy was the "Brief Problem-Solving Therapy" model developed by the Mental Research Institute (MRI) in Palo Alto, California (Watzlawick, Weakland, and Fisch, 1974; Weakland, Fisch, and Watzlawick, 1974). Focusing on understanding the interaction and communication patterns between people, the MRI team essentially conceived of problems as "failed solution attempts" which were reinforced and maintained in patterns of family communications. For example, a mother in an effort to get close to her son may bombard him with questions when he comes home from school. But this approach may have the opposite effect and cause him to pull away. The aim of MRI therapy is to identify these patterns and to help the family "do something different," even if it is simply the opposite of what was done before. In the last example, the mother may find a solution by waiting for her son's initiative to communicate and then listen, rather than bombard him as before. Although the solution-focused therapy model shifted to consider solution rather than problem development (de Shazer et al., 1986), the model built on the basic approach of the MRI team. For example, it evolved the "three rules" of therapy and "problem solving" as:

1. If it's not broken, don't fix it.
2. Once you know what works, do more of it.
3. If it doesn't work, don't do it again; do something different. (Berg and Miller, 1992)

These rules apply not only to problems that exist in clients' lives, but also to the therapeutic process itself. The therapist should continually be sensitive to feedback from the client about what is working in the therapy, for example, what questions are most helpful, or what format the session should take (e.g., whether a client should be seen with his or her partner or alone). A common path to therapeutic stuckness occurs when the therapist, in the face of failing therapy, continues to "do more of the same" intervention in the hope that it will yield a different result. If a client becomes more suicidal following a number of individual therapy sessions, the therapist may increase the frequency of the sessions, rather than change the format of the sessions (e.g., considering family or couple work). Or when medication prescribed for depression is not working, a patient may be offered increased levels of the drug rather than an alternative form of treatment. The central rule "If it doesn't work, don't do it again; do something different" needs to be applied in these instances.

When the Theory Doesn't Fit

Sometimes other factors lead to difficulties in the therapeutic alliance, as in "theory counter-transference" (Duncan, Hubble, and Miller, 1997). This is essentially a clash between the therapist's beliefs and model of therapy and the client's expectations and preferred method of therapy. Suppose a client who had been sexually abused as a child has a strong desire to disclose and tell her story of abuse. If she goes to a solution-focused therapist who doesn't listen to her story and keeps asking her what the future might be like when she has dealt with the abuse, she is likely to feel misunderstood. Or suppose it is a different client who was also sexually abused, but has the opposite desire of putting it behind her. If she goes to a psychodynamic therapist she is likely to be viewed as being in denial and the therapy could falter. Joining with clients means also joining with their worldviews, trying to understand their expectations for therapy, and adapting your style accordingly. When a clash of client expectations and therapeutic techniques occurs, it is generally best to discuss this openly with the client in a nondefensive way. For example, in the aforementioned first case of sexual abuse, the therapist could open the discussion in the following way:

THERAPIST: I really want to make these meetings helpful to you . . . so can I check something out with you?

CLIENT: Sure.

THERAPIST: When a person has suffered a trauma in childhood like you have, some people say it is a good idea to talk about what has happened to help them deal with it. Other people say it is best to try to concentrate on the future and on getting over it. Other people say a mixture of both is best. What do you think would be best for you?

CLIENT: Mmm, I don't know . . . I do want to talk about it, to get it off my chest, but it is painful. I don't want to dwell on it and let it get me down. I do want to put it behind me and move on.

THERAPIST: How much do you need to tell me about what happened so you can move on?

CLIENT: I'm not sure. I do want to tell you about it so you know and it's not a secret anymore.

THERAPIST: I understand. . . . . You want to break the silence so it's not a secret, yet you don't want to overly dwell on it. . . . . Can I make a suggestion?

CLIENT: Please.

THERAPIST: Tell me as much as you feel would help you. If you're unsure, we can pause and you don't have to tell me anything if you are not comfortable. If I ask a question that you don't want to answer then just tell me and I'll try and ask a better one! [Client smiles.] Is that OK?

Being transparent about the techniques of therapy and negotiating with the client how to proceed is a very effective way of establishing an alliance with the client as well as ensuring the therapy makes progress. It gives the client the opportunity to buy into the process and to share the responsibility for what happens next. Done well, it is an opportunity for the therapist to communicate that he or she is on the client's side and that the therapeutic model serves the client rather than the other way around. A good solution-focused therapist should be flexible enough to adapt to the client's wishes and unique way of cooperating, even if it means abandoning the solution-focused model if required.

Staying a Customer As a Therapist

The deductive mind never rests. It's not unlike a finely tuned musical instrument, which demands attention and practice.

Sherlock Holmes

Practice Exercise 6.1.
Supervision Exercise with a Difficult Case

The purpose of this supervision exercise is to generate ideas to help you move forward on a case where you feel stuck as a therapist. The aim is to try to think differently about the situation by discovering new strengths and possibilities, both within the client's resources and within your own approach to the client.

Think about a case that you are having difficulty with and begin to consider the following questions which may help you to think differently.

1. Thinking constructively about the client

   - What strengths about the client does the impasse reveal?
   - What positive client intentions underlie the client's actions?
   - What is his or her level of motivation? (visitor? complainant?) How can you adapt your approach to accommodate this?
   - Despite the stuckness, what is going well for this client? How is he or she coping with his or her difficulties?
   - What do you like and admire about this client?
   - What positive goals/aspirations does the client have that are not the subject of the therapy but which could be?
   - What resources and strengths does he or she have access or potential access to?
   - Who are the supporters/helpers of the client not considered previously?

2. Thinking constructively about your practice

   - What are you aiming for in the work that your client is not aiming for?
   - What goals/methods of work do you agree upon with the client?
   - What strengths does this impasse reveal about your work as a therapist?
   - What is going well in your work with this client or in his or her contact with professional services? What has gone well in the past?
   - What are you doing constructively as a therapist in spite of any difficulties or the current impasse?
   - What resources and strengths do you have as a therapist that might be helpful to this client?

One of the great appeals of solution-focused therapy is the fact that its principles are simple and concise. However, such simplicity does not mean that the principles are always easy to apply in practice or to sustain in the face of difficult contexts. It is one thing to be respectful, optimistic, curious, and flexible in a well resourced agency with clients who are largely at the customer level of motivation. It is quite another thing to maintain a respectful, constructive stance in a context in which clients are largely at the visitor or complainant level of motivation and you are in a very underfunded agency where you feel undervalued and unsupported, or worse still, if high levels of conflict are evident (either within the agency or outside). In these instances it is easy to become burned out or pessimistic.

To be constantly constructive, optimistic, and respectful requires great energy and flexibility on the part of the therapist. Encountering difficult situations can cause this to wane. We can easily be overcome by negative feelings for our clients and feel hopeless about the possibility of progress. Certain clients and certain situations can stir up our "own stuff" and we can be taken over by negative emotions and memories that make us less effective. Just as it is easy for clients to slip into complainant or visitor levels of motivation about their goals, so can therapists slip into visitor or complainant levels of motivation toward their own therapeutic work. For example, therapists become visitors when they feel detached or disinterested in their work or clients; they become complainants when they feel pessimistic about change and hopeless about being effective. If this happens, therapists do not have the optimism and energy to take on difficult cases. It is therefore crucial for therapists to take steps to monitor and maintain

their own mental health and resourcefulness, and to ensure that they stay as customers to their work.

If you find yourself slipping to the "complainant" level of motivation toward your own work, it is important to pause, take time to reflect, and to highlight your own self-care and seek support. Supervision and consultation with colleagues is critical in this respect. Indeed, we have found that consulting with colleagues and working as part of a team which can provide support and constructive understanding when the going gets tough is the single biggest factor in preserving our ability to be effective therapists. Consider also Practice Exercise 6.2 to help you identify personal and professional resources which can sustain you as a therapist. This is an exercise that can be adapted for clients.

Practice Exercise 6.2. Achieving Balance

Self-care and personal renewal are about achieving balance in your life. They try to ensure that you address your different needs in a balanced way each week. There are four dimensions of personal renewal that we need to address weekly in order to have a balanced and stress-free life.

Work through the following list identifying things you do that sustain and renew you as a person and professional. Note any areas where you feel you are not taking enough action.

1. Physical:
   Exercise (such as walking, jogging, playing sports)
   Eating well and healthily
   Getting good rest and relaxation
2. Mental:
   Keeping your mind stimulated with other interests (such as reading, movies, theater, etc.)
   Learning new things
3. Emotional:
   Keeping in contact with friends. Connecting with intimate family (such as a special night out with your partner)
   Doing self-nurturing things (such as treating yourself to a special bath or a shopping trip)
4. Spiritual:
   Time alone or in nature
   Time for personal reflection
   Meditation, prayer
   Goal setting, reconnecting to your values

Summary

In this chapter, we have acknowledged that the task of the solution-focused detective is not always easy and often the cases we work with can become stuck or appear to go against us. We described some of the "dead ends" we can easily travel down, such as misunderstanding the clients' motivation, doing more of the same in the face of failure, and letting our own theory get in the way of helping the client. We gave suggestions as to how each of these obstacles can be overcome and how we can get back on the right track to making progress with our clients. Finally, we discussed how important you, the therapist, are in successful therapy. We highlighted how critical it is to prioritize your own self-care as a professional, via good supervision, consultation, and training (and whatever else works for you) to ensure you "stay as a customer" in your work. It is your ongoing ability to be empathic and constructive with clients in the face of problems, to constantly seek to understand and ally with them no matter how bad things are, that is your greatest resource in finding a way forward.

A Final Note

A solution-focused goal is not the end but the beginning of something new. Progress opens up new possibilities and new goals and an ongoing cycle of improvement and change. Although we have come to the end of our book and our description of the solution journey, we believe it is also another beginning. We hope it has been a step in the right direction in your ongoing development as therapist and professional. Just as the art of deduction employed by a detective cannot be reduced to a set of techniques, but is exemplified by the personal qualities of the detective, the work of a solution-focused therapist is not simply specific techniques or questions, but the foundation is a respectful, empathic, and curious attitude on the part of the therapist. The idea is to direct your curiosity to where clients want to go rather than where they have been, to what they do right rather than what they do wrong, and to encourage them to become the expert in their own life.

We hope this respectful spirit has permeated this book as we encourage you to recognize the strengths that already exist in your own practice and abilities as a therapist. We know that there is no right way to do therapy; we must merely follow some guiding principles. (Indeed, the three of us have such different styles that we sometimes wonder what we have in common!) We encourage you to create your own style and to take steps to discover that works in your practice with your clients. When you do, make sure to do more of it.

Appendix

Key to Case Studies

The suggestions and ideas in this section are by no means complete or comprehensive. They merely represent a few ideas that we believed might be helpful to the case in question. We expect that you will generate far more creative, interesting, and relevant ideas. Our hope is that the exercises will provoke you to think deeply about your cases and to find new ways that build on your current strengths as a therapist. Remember there are no right or wrong answers to cases, only creative ideas that may be useful in moving the case forward. The final arbiters are the clients; listen carefully for their feedback.

Case Study 1.1

1. Mary has four children, a relatively large family. It takes considerable skill to parent such a family. What has she learned? What skills does she find most useful? Which aspects of parenting does she perform well?

2. The referral only mentions problems with the youngest child. Perhaps some of the other children are doing well in school or elsewhere. It is worth asking Mary about these children and what is going well in their lives, so she can reveal aspects of her parenting that are beneficial and for which she can take credit. Can some of these skills perhaps be transferred to caring for the youngest child?

3. Mary is sensitive to criticism. This suggests that she is proud of her parenting and that being a good parent is something she both values and strives toward. It would be worth exploring her ideal of parenting. What does she think is important about bringing up children? What values does she hold? What are her goals for her children?

4. What has Mary learned from her own experience of childhood? How did she cope with the abuse she suffered? What would she like to be different for her children? What parts of her childhood were rewarding? Who was there for her at that time? What would she like to preserve from her childhood?

5. Mary has had much previous contact with professional services and has knowledge of how these relationships can go wrong. Therefore, she has ideas about the type of professional contact she would like and what might work best for her. (Even her descriptions of negative interactions with services will provide you with clues as to how she might act differently.) It would be worthwhile to investigate which professional services were most helpful to her in the past. What worked well? What would she like to change?

6. Mary is an "on and off" alcoholic. During what periods has she been able to manage sobriety? How has she achieved this? Where does she find the strength to stop drinking? What supports help her?

7. Mary attends a community education course, which is no mean achievement given that she is also a mother of four children. It is worth exploring her motivation to do this. This may reveal a desire to better herself and her family, shows great organizational skills at managing a busy life, and provides potential support networks both at the college and in her community. She may be able to tap into these strengths and resources to solve her other problems.

Case Study 2.1

1. What model or method would you have used in the past to connect with Max and his problems? If you were trying to integrate solution-focused ideas into your work, how would you integrate listening to Max's painful past with giving him hope for the future? We often ask clients how they feel their lives would be different in the present if they were to talk about or resolve their problems from the past. Often, people have clear ideas that they want something to change now if they sort out their past. Already Max is talking about the preferred future including a romantic relationship. Could this be followed up to explore more of what Max wants as he begins to move on from his past?

2. Max has coped and survived his past up to this point. Questions could be asked that give Max credit for surviving a difficult childhood and understand the qualities he has that allowed him to manage up to this point.

3. Max can also be given credit for choosing to come to therapy. He has been able to tap into his friendship and use this helpful relationship to seek assistance in changing. He may have hopes that this start, coming to therapy, will cause bigger changes that will make his life more fulfilling.

4. It is possible to balance talking about the past and the future with clients. We often ask clients what they feel would be useful. Questions include: "Do you think it would be useful to talk about your past and what happened to you or would you prefer to talk about how you would like your life to change because of being here?" "If we do talk about your past, how will that

be helpful to you now?" These types of questions allow the client to make the choice regarding past or future talk. They also begin to establish a perceived benefit to the client for the often difficult task of talking about the past.

5. The areas of Max's life that he is currently happy with could be explored, or problem-free talk in solution-focused terms. These current life successes may help to establish with Max that he is moving forward in some areas of his life and that insight may help him progress in other areas of his life, such as the relationship he desires. If Max becomes more aware of his strengths and resources, he may be able to use them in other areas of his life.

6. The use of humor is difficult to gauge unless you are in the therapeutic room with the client. Many factors indicate to therapists that they may be able to share a smile or laugh with a client at a particularly tense time. The risk of humor is very difficult to judge when reading a case on paper; clients' facial expressions, body language, and voice inflections all need to be considered. We believe that this call can only be made when two people are interacting and a relationship has been formed.

Case Study 3.1

Example A

THERAPIST: Rick, welcome! How do you think I might be able to help you here today?

RICK: [Shrugging shoulders] Don't know.

THERAPIST: I understand that it was your parole officer's idea for you to come. Is that right?

RICK: Yeah, he suggested that I should come.

THERAPIST: What do you think would need to happen here for him to think that your attending was useful?

RICK: I'm not sure. I guess he would like to see me not getting into fights and trouble with the police.

THERAPIST: And for you what would be helpful?

RICK: I guess to get him off my back would be good. Not getting myself into fights would be better. I'm sick of all the hassle recently. It seems every time I go out there is a fight.

Example B

THERAPIST: How do you think I might be able to help you here today?

SALLY: [Tearful] I just don't know. I'm so upset, everything is crashing down around me and . . . [more tears].

THERAPIST: [Handing a tissue to Sally] Sounds like things have been pretty tough for you lately.

SALLY: My life was going fine. I was hanging out, studying, my friends, boyfriend, I was great. Then it all changed last week, after the attack. I'm just staying in and not doing anything now. I can't do anything.

THERAPIST: So your life was going really well and now you feel things have stopped for the moment?

SALLY: Yeah, I'm just very scared now . . . and angry that this happened to me.

THERAPIST: Sounds hard.

SALLY: Yeah, I just don't want to be scared anymore. Scared of leaving the house or who might be out there.

THERAPIST: I see. And if you weren't scared anymore what would you be doing?

SALLY: I guess I would get back to the things I used to do.

THERAPIST: Could you tell me a little bit about what you used to enjoy doing?

Case Study 4.1

1. Sue has a sense of herself in the past as a capable woman. She talks about being proud of her accomplishments at work and about her supportive family and friends. How could you help Sue to rethink her past experiences and to look at the strengths and abilities that she feels have helped her through?

2. The psychiatrist working with Sue has seen an improvement over the past week, demonstrated by Sue's discharge from the hospital and referral to day treatment services. Sue's improvement in keeping herself safe and a demonstration to the psychiatrist of this safety could be explored. The search for improvements that have already occurred is called presession change.

3. Sue also mentions that she has been open with family and friends regarding her situation and that this openness has encouraged people to offer their support and help. Could discussion with Sue regarding her ability to access support encourage her continuation of improvement in these areas?

4. Sue has a mixed description of her past, with times of both achievement and loneliness. Looking for exceptions or times in her life when she felt she was not lonely may give the therapist insight into the things that help Sue feel supported.

5. This is the first suicide attempt that Sue has made. How has she been able to cope with difficult times in the past in a way that did not lead her to

harm herself? How could you encourage Sue to notice and repeat behaviors that helped her feel less lonely and in control of "spinning downward"?

6. Scaling might be creatively used to find out how far Sue has come since she made the suicide attempt. The psychiatrist has noticed improvement; it would be interesting to find out if Sue believes that she is feeling safer than the week she was admitted to the hospital.

7. A discussion of the benefits of Sue addressing her loneliness and depression in a way that does not involve harming herself might allow her to link the positive aspects of finding a better way to cope with the difficult times in her life.

Case Study 5.1

1. The family came to counseling together; this could be feedback as a sign of their desire for change.

2. Family members each talk about things becoming worse over the past few months. This may be an indication that they at one time related positively. Would it be appropriate to feed this back to them?

3. Mr. Miller expresses his love and concern for his children. How can this be used to encourage the family to work toward a better future together?

4. Mrs. Miller states that she would be "heartbroken" if her husband left. She clearly would like to find a way to improve the situation at home and continue to live with her husband.

5. The children express love for their father during the session. How can this be fed back to the family in a useful way?

6. The family seem to have the mutual goal of wanting to stay living together as a family, without continuous fights.

Many possible homework assignments could be given. One possibility would be to ask the family to notice the times they relate well to one another and do not fight.

Case Study 6.1

Example A: Teenager—Visitor; Mother—Complainant

1. The teenager should be welcomed and invited into the therapy. Spend time getting to know his hobbies, interests, strengths, and what is going well in his life. He can also be complimented for his cooperative actions thus far—coming to therapy despite his reservations—a possible sign of empathy with his mother or a willingness to negotiate. He may become a customer if the therapy focuses on a different goal. He may not be motivated at

this point to stop using drugs but is very motivated to regain his independence from his parents. The question could become "what can I do to help convince my parents that I am safe"?

2. The mother in the example should receive empathy (finding her son using drugs) and complimented for her ability to take action (coming to therapy) because it reveals her love for her son and desire to be a good parent. She may move from being a complainant if she rediscovers her power and influence over her son. She may recall a time she was able to "get through" to her son or when drug abuse was not a problem in the family. If these exceptions are identified and she can take some responsibility for them, she is on the road to being a customer.

Example B: Wife—Complainant; Husband—Complainant

Both currently explain their difficulties in terms of the other's behavior, expecting the other to change. The therapist could empathize with the difficulties they individually and collectively face in their marriage in a way that focuses on possibilities and does not take sides:

THERAPIST: [Addressing wife] You want your husband to spend more time at home and to be more affectionate. That is important to you. [Addressing husband] You want your wife to be less critical toward you, perhaps to appreciate you more and what you do well . . . is that right?

The therapist could then try to achieve a workable common goal for the therapy, one they feel equally responsible for and which they are willing to work for.

THERAPIST: So, what are your hopes for these meetings? What would you both like to achieve?

When this is established, the therapist can then help the couple expand this in concrete, interpersonal detail.

THERAPIST: So suppose your marriage is going better. What will be different? How will you both behave differently to each other?

Remember, when working with couples it is important that you do not assume you know that the goal is to make the marriage work. Often a more preliminary goal is necessary first; for example, the couple may have to decide whether they are going to stay together.

References

Ansbacher, H. L. and Ansbacher, R. R. (Eds.) (1998). *Individual psychology of Alfred Adler: A systematic presentation in selections from his writings.* New York: HarperCollins.

Baum, F. L. (1998). *The wonderful world of Oz.* New York: Penguin.

Beck, A. (1976). *Cognitive therapy and emotional disorders.* New York: International Universities Press.

Berg, I. K. (1991). *Family preservation: A brief therapy workbook.* London: Brief Therapy Press.

Berg, I. K. (1994). *Family-based services: A solution-focused approach.* New York: W.W. Norton.

Berg, I. K. and Miller, S. D. (1992). *Working with the problem drinker: A solution-focused approach.* New York: W.W. Norton.

Beyebach, M., Morejon, A. R., Palenzuela, D. L., and Rodriguez-Arias, J. L. (1996). Research on the process of solution-focused therapy. In S. D. Miller, M. A. Hubble, and B. L. Duncan (Eds.), *Handbook of solution focused brief therapy.* San Francisco: Jossey-Bass.

Boldt, L. G. (1997). *Zen Soup: Tasty morsels of wisdom from great minds East and West.* New York: Penguin.

Capaccione, L. (1979). *The creative journal: The art of finding yourself.* Athens, OH: Ohio University/Swallow Press.

Carroll, L. (1992). *Alice's adventures in Wonderland.* Hong Kong: Red Fox.

Conan Doyle, A. (1998). *The complete Sherlock Holmes: All four novels and fifty-six short stories.* Bantam Doubleday.

Conan Doyle, A. (2001). Sherlock Holmes—The science of deduction and analysis. Available at <http://members.nbci.com/peterjim/sherlockholmes/>, Dimitrios Markatos, August 16, 2001.

de Shazer, S. (1984). The imaginary pill technique. *Journal of Strategic and Systemic Therapies, 3*(1), 30-34.

de Shazer, S. (1985). *Keys to solution in brief therapy.* New York: W.W. Norton.

de Shazer, S. (1988). *Clues: Investigating solutions in brief therapy.* New York: W.W. Norton.

de Shazer, S., Berg, I. K., Lipchik, E., Nunnally, F., Molnar, A., Gingerich, W. J., and Weiner-Davis, M. (1986). Brief therapy: Focused solution development. *Family Process, 25,* 207-221.

Duncan, B. L., Hubble, M. A., and Miller, S. D. (1997). *Psychotherapy with "impossible" cases: The efficient treatment of therapy veterans.* New York: W.W. Norton.

Duncan, B. L. and Miller, S. D. (2000). *The heroic client: Doing client-directed, outcome-informed therapy.* San Francisco: Jossey-Bass.

Ellis, A. (1998). How rational-emotive therapy belongs to the constructivist camp. In M. Hoyt (Ed.), *The handbook of constructive therapies* (pp. 83-99). San Francisco: Jossey-Bass.

Erickson, M. H. and Rossi, E. (1980). *Innovative hypnotherapy: Collected papers of Milton Erickson on hypnosis.* New York: Irvington.

Freud, S. (1949). *An outline of psychoanalysis.* New York: W.W. Norton.

Friedman, S. (1995). *The reflecting team in action: Collaborative practice in family therapy.* New York: Guilford Press.

Furman, B. and Ahola, T. (1992). *Solution talk: Hosting therapeutic conversations.* New York: W.W. Norton.

Furman, B. and Ahola, T. (1997). *Succeeding together: Solution-oriented team building.* Helsinki: International Reteaming Institute <www.reteaming.com>.

Garfield, S. and Bergin, A. (1994). *Handbook of psychotherapy and behavior change* (Fourth edition). New York: Wiley.

George, E. (1998). Solution-focused therapy training seminar. Maynooth, Ireland.

George, E., Iveson, C., Ratner, H. (1990). *Problem to solution.* London: Brief Therapy Press.

Gergen, K. J. and McNamee, S. (Eds.) (1992). *Therapy as social construction.* London: Sage.

Harrington, W. (1996). *The game show killer.* New York: Forge.

Hoyt, M. F. (1998). *The handbook of constructive therapies: Innovative approaches from leading practitioners.* San Francisco: Jossey-Bass.

Hubble, M. L., Duncan, B. L., and Miller, S. D. (1999). *The heart and soul of change: What works in therapy.* Washington, DC: American Psychological Association.

Lazarus, A. A. (1989). *The practice of multi-modal therapy.* Baltimore: John Hopkins University Press.

Lethem, J. (1994). *Moved to tears, moved to action: Solution-focused brief therapy with women and children.* London: Brief Therapy Press.

Lipchik, E. (1994). The rush to be brief. *Networker* (March/April), 35-39.

McKeel, A. J. (1996). A clinician's guide to research on solution-focused brief therapy. In S. D. Miller, M. A. Hubble, and B. L. Duncan (Eds.), *Handbook of solution-focused brief therapy* (pp. 251-271). San Francisco: Jossey-Bass.

Miller, S. D. (1998). *Psychotherapy with impossible cases.* Paper presented at the Brief Therapy Conference, Dublin, Ireland.

Miller, S. D., Duncan, B. L., and Hubble, M. A. (1997). *Escape from Babel: Toward a unifying language for psychotherapy practice.* New York: W.W. Norton.

Minuchin, S. (1974). *Families and family therapy*. Cambridge, MA: Harvard University Press.

Minuchin, S., Montalvo, B., Guerney, B. G., Dosman, B. L., and Schumer, B. G. (1967). *Families of the slums*. New York: Basic Books.

Nylund, D. and Corsiglia, V. (1994). Becoming solution-forced in brief therapy: Remembering something important we already knew. *Journal of Systemic Therapies, 13*(1), 5-12.

O'Connell, B. (1998). *Solution-focused therapy*. London: Sage.

Prochaska, J. O. and DiClemente, C. C. (1992). The transtheoretical approach. In J. C. Norcross and M. R. Goldfried (Eds.), *Handbook of psychotherapy integration* (pp. 300-334). New York: Basic Books.

Prochaska, J. O., DiClemente, C. C., and Norcross, J. C. (1992). In search of how people change: Applications to addictive behaviors. *American Psychologist, 47*(9), 1102-1114.

Rogers, C. R. (1961). *On becoming a person: A therapist's view of psychotherapy*. London: Constable.

Rogers, C. R. (1986). Client-centered therapy. In I. L. Kutash and A. Wolf (Eds.), *Psychotherapist's casebook* (pp. 197-208). San Francisco: Jossey-Bass.

Selekman, M. D. (1997). *Solution-focused therapy with children: Harnessing family strengths for systemic change*. New York: Guilford Press.

Sharry, J. (1999). *Bringing up responsible children*. Dublin: Veritas.

Sharry, J. (2001). *Solution-focused groupwork*. London: Sage.

Sharry, J. and Fitzpatrick, C. (2001). Parents Plus Families and Adolescents Programme: A video-based guide to managing conflict and getting on better with older children and teenagers aged 11-16: Parents Plus, c/o Mater Child Guidance Clinic, Mater Hospital, North Circular Road, Dublin 7, Ireland. Available at <www.brieftherapy.ie/parentsplus>.

Sharry, J., Madden, B., Darmody, M., and Miller, S. D. (2001). Giving our clients the break: Applications of client-directed outcome-informed clinical work. *Journal of Systemic Therapies, 20*(3), 68-76.

Sharry, J., Reid, P., and Donohoe, E. (2001). *When parents separate: A guide to helping you and your children cope*. Dublin: Veritas.

Van Bilsen, H. P. J. G. (1991). Motivational interviewing: Perspectives from the Netherlands, with particular emphasis on heroin-dependent clients. In W. R. Miller and S. Rollnick (Eds.), *Motivational interviewing: Preparing people to change addictive behavior*. New York: Guilford Press.

Wade, A. (1997). Small acts of living: Everyday resistance to violence and other forms of oppression. *Contemporary Family Therapy, 19*(1), 23-39.

Walter, J. and Peller, J. (2000). *Recreating brief therapy*. New York: W.W. Norton.

Watzlawick, P., Weakland, J., and Fisch, R. (1974). *Change: Principles of problem formation and problem resolution*. New York: W.W. Norton.

Weakland, J., Fisch, R., and Watzlawick, P. (1974). Brief therapy: Focused problem resolution. *Family Process, 13,* 141-168.

Weiner-Davis, M., de Shazer, S., and Gingerich, W. J. (1987). Building on the pre-treatment change to construct the therapeutic solution: An exploratory study. *Journal of Marital and Family Therapy,* 13, 359-365.

White, M. and Epston, D. (1990). *Narrative means to therapeutic ends.* New York: W.W. Norton.

Index

Page numbers followed by the letter "t" indicate a table.

SPECIAL 25%-OFF DISCOUNT!
Order a copy of this book with this form or online at:
http://www.haworthpressinc.com/store/product.asp?sku=4862

BECOMING A SOLUTION DETECTIVE
Identifying Your Clients' Strengths in Practical Brief Therapy

_____in hardbound at $29.96 (regularly $39.95) (ISBN: 0-7890-1833-0)

_____in softbound at $14.96 (regularly $19.95) (ISBN: 0-7890-1834-9)

Or order online and use Code HEC25 in the shopping cart.

COST OF BOOKS_____

OUTSIDE US/CANADA/
MEXICO: ADD 20%_____

POSTAGE & HANDLING_____
*(US: $5.00 for first book & $2.00
for each additional book)
Outside US: $6.00 for first book
& $2.00 for each additional book)*

SUBTOTAL_____

IN CANADA: ADD 7% GST_____

STATE TAX_____
*(NY, OH & MN residents, please
add appropriate local sales tax)*

FINAL TOTAL_____
*(If paying in Canadian funds,
convert using the current
exchange rate, UNESCO
coupons welcome)*

☐ **BILL ME LATER:** ($5 service charge will be added)
(Bill-me option is good on US/Canada/Mexico orders only;
not good to jobbers, wholesalers, or subscription agencies.)

☐ Check here if billing address is different from
shipping address and attach purchase order and
billing address information.

Signature_____

☐ **PAYMENT ENCLOSED: $**_____

☐ **PLEASE CHARGE TO MY CREDIT CARD.**

☐ Visa ☐ MasterCard ☐ AmEx ☐ Discover
☐ Diner's Club ☐ Eurocard ☐ JCB

Account # _____

Exp. Date_____

Signature_____

Prices in US dollars and subject to change without notice.

NAME_____

INSTITUTION_____

ADDRESS_____

CITY_____

STATE/ZIP_____

COUNTRY_____ COUNTY (NY residents only)_____

TEL_____ FAX_____

E-MAIL_____

May we use your e-mail address for confirmations and other types of information? ☐ Yes ☐ No
We appreciate receiving your e-mail address and fax number. Haworth would like to e-mail or fax special
discount offers to you, as a preferred customer. **We will never share, rent, or exchange your e-mail address
or fax number.** We regard such actions as an invasion of your privacy.

Order From Your Local Bookstore or Directly From
The Haworth Press, Inc.
10 Alice Street, Binghamton, New York 13904-1580 • USA
TELEPHONE: 1-800-HAWORTH (1-800-429-6784) / Outside US/Canada: (607) 722-5857
FAX: 1-800-895-0582 / Outside US/Canada: (607) 722-6362
E-mail to: getinfo@haworthpressinc.com
PLEASE PHOTOCOPY THIS FORM FOR YOUR PERSONAL USE.
http://www.HaworthPress.com
BOF02